Screaming Hawk Returns

Critical acclaim for *Screaming Hawk*

Patton Boyle crafts a completely surprising narrative about a true conversion experience and its inescapable paradoxes. As a Christian at mid-life foundering in dry religion, his hero learns to fly and scream like a hawk under the tutelage of a wry Native American teacher, who shares his hard-won secrets, shows us how to reset the boundaries of self, belief, and Spirit, and shape new life.

Richard Leviton
Author of *Looking for Arthur: A Once and Future Travelogue,*
editor of *Alternative Medicine*

A wonderful book, filled with insights into the spiritual life, Native American spirituality, teaching, and learning.

The Rev. John H. Westerhoff III
Author of *Will Our Children Have Faith?*,
retired Professor of Theology and Christian Nurture, Duke University

Spiritually beautiful and exciting — it all seems too fantastic for words, yet too real to deny.

The Rev. Donald L. Keefauver
United Methodist Church, retired

A spiritually beautiful book filled with insights into the spiritual life and the paradoxes which appear in religious beliefs.

Southern Book Trade

Screaming Hawk Returns

FLYING EAGLE TEACHES THE MYSTIC PATHS

Patton Boyle

Station Hill Press

Published by Station Hill Press, Inc. Barrytown, New York 12507, for Station Hill Literary Editions, under the Institute for Publishing Arts, Inc., Barrytown, New York 12507. Station Hill Literary Editions is supported in part by grants from the National Endowment for the Arts, a Federal Agency in Washington, D.C., and by the New York State Council on the Arts.

Distributed by the Talman Company, 131 Spring Street, Suite 201 E-N, New York, New York 10012.

Front cover painting by Stephen Hickman.
Cover design by Susan Quasha and Vicki Hickman.
Book design by Susan Quasha and Alison Wilkes.

Library of Congress Cataloging-in-Publication Data

Boyle, Patton L.
    Screaming Hawk Returns:Flying Eagle Teaches the Mystic Paths / Patton Boyle
        p. cm.
    ISBN 0-88268-192-3
        1. Indians of North America—Religion—Fiction. 2. Spiritual life—Fiction. I. Title.
    PS3552.0929S36   1997
    813'.54—dc20
                                                                95-19718
                                                                CIP

Manufactured in the United States of America.

Author's Preface

What follows is the account of Screaming Hawk's second summer of training under Flying Eagle, a Native American medicine man. Although many may choose to do so, it is not necessary to have read *Screaming Hawk: Flying Eagle's Training of a Mystic Warrior* in order to understand the teachings contained in this second phase of Screaming Hawk's instruction.

As with the first Screaming Hawk book, in many respects this book is not my own creation. At no point in the process of writing it did I have any outline and most of the time I had no awareness of what the next sentence or, at times, even the next word would be. The words simply came and the teachings and story unfolded essentially as they are presented here. At times, I was surprised by Flying Eagle's teachings and did not agree with some of them as they came forth. But over time, I have come to experience the truth of his teachings on a deeper level and I now agree with all of them.

The Spirit speaks to me in this book. But do not look for the truth in the words themselves. Flying Eagle cautions his student not to look for the truth in his words, but "in the silence between the words." May you too hear in the silence between the words.

Screaming Hawk Returns

❧ 1 ❧

As I climbed out of my car I heard the commotion.

"You are dumb, stupid and crazy if you think I am going to put up with this, Flying Eagle! I didn't come all this way to have you insult me!" she shouted.

"I can identify with the third adjective," said Flying Eagle calmly. "The mere fact that I am a medicine man puts me in that category for some people, but I am having a little trouble with the first two. But perhaps I am too dumb or too stupid to see that I am dumb and stupid."

"Don't play word games with me, you God damned pig-headed bastard! I'm leaving! And you can go to Hell for all I care!" She turned abruptly and stormed down the front steps of Flying Eagle's lodge, her golden hair flying in the breeze as she blazed a path to her torch red Stingray convertible and threw open the door. She paused only long enough to flash an obscene gesture in the direction of Flying Eagle, who had, in the meantime, seated himself comfortably in a rustic looking chair on his porch. Flying Eagle observed her parting shot but did not react to it. She threw herself behind the steering wheel, furiously slammed the door, and then roared out of the parking area amid a shower of flying dirt, dust and pine needles.

It was then that Flying Eagle saw me standing beside my car. Instantly he broke into a wide grin that smoothed out some of the wrinkles in his octogenarian face and came rushing toward me like a man in his 20's.

"Screaming Hawk," he cried, using the Indian name he had given me the previous summer, "it is good to see you!" He gave me a bear hug and slapped me on the back. "I was hoping you would arrive today. "You look well. Did you have a good trip out here?"

"Oh, it was mixed. But it's great to see you, Flying Eagle. I've really missed you.

"What was that?" I asked, gesturing in the direction of the dust cloud that was still settling.

"Oh, that. That was the conclusion of an interview I was having with a young woman who said she wanted to become my student."

"From what I saw, Flying Eagle, she didn't seem very impressed with you."

"No, I don't think she was."

"What did you say to her, if you don't mind my asking?"

"No, not at all. I merely told her that she must have me confused with her rich Daddy if she thinks she can just sit there and bat her eyes and charm me into giving her what she wants."

"And that's all you said?"

"Well, that and a few insulting precursors. But that was essentially what I told her. She did not take it well."

"Obviously," I said, looking back at the dust cloud.

"It is amazing how a few carefully placed insults can sort out those who merely think our religion is interesting from those who are really serious about learning the ways of the Spirit. She drove here all the way from Chicago and lasted only 37 minutes. It's a shame, good students are hard to come by."

He looked at me with a cold, hard stare. "And what about you? Back for another summer of abuse from the crazy old medicine man?"

"Something like that," I said, trying to look solemn.

His expression shifted to a good natured smile. "It's good to see you, Screaming Hawk. When I got your letter saying you would like to come back this summer, I was very pleased. I have never had a student quite like you. I have grown rather fond of you, despite the fact that you still have a very thick skull," he said, tapping me on the side of the head with his finger. "Let's take a walk, I want to hear about your trip out here."

We headed down one of the forest trails we had traveled so many times during Flying Eagle's teaching sessions the previous summer. It felt wonderful to be back in the forest again. We walked in silence for a few minutes as I absorbed all the familiar sights and smells. When we came to a fallen tree beside the trail, Flying Eagle suggested that we sit and talk there.

"Well. Aren't you going to tell me about your trip?" he said after we sat down.

"There isn't really much to tell, just lots of long, tedious, hours on the road."

"Did anything happen that was different?"

"No. Just a flat tire. That's all."

"Tell me all about it."

"Why do you want to hear about that, Flying Eagle?"

"Tell me all about it," he said again.

"O.K. It was last night. I had gotten bored with the Interstate and had been driving on a parallel highway for a couple of hours. I've found that driving through a small town now and then can help break the monotony."

"Tell me about the flat tire, Screaming Hawk."

"I'm getting to that. An hour or two after dark it started to rain pretty hard. I had the windshield wipers going full speed but the visibility still wasn't very good. As I came around a little bend I saw something lying across most of the road. I'm still not sure what it was, probably one of those metal bands shippers put around packing cases. Anyway, I saw it too late to stop. I slowed down as much as I could and tried to swerve around it but I ran over part of it with my right tires. Everything seemed O.K. at first but after a mile or so I noticed the car pulling harder and harder to the right. I stopped and got out."

"In the rain?" he asked with a sly grin.

"Yes, in the rain. I got out and checked the tire. Sure enough, the right front tire was leaking air through a little gash in it. By that time it was too flat to continue driving on it."

Flying Eagle chuckled.

"I unloaded the trunk."

"In the rain," Flying Eagle added.

"Yes. In the rain. I unloaded the trunk but I couldn't find the jack handle."

Flying Eagle laughed.

"I put everything back in the trunk and decided to walk to a service station."

"In the rain."

"Yes, Flying Eagle, in the rain."

"Because nobody came along to help."

"How did you know?"

"Please go on," he said laughing.

"I walked to a service station."

"How far was it?"

"About two miles. And when I got there it was closed."

He slapped his leg and roared with laughter.

"Damn it, Flying Eagle! I don't see anything funny about that."

"You wouldn't, Screaming Hawk. So what did you do next?"

"Well, the pay phone was out of order..."

"Of course," said Flying Eagle under his breath.

"...so I ended up spending a miserable night in a storage shed behind the service station. I got help when the station opened in the morning."

"And did you ever find the jack handle?"

"Yes. This morning. It was under the front seat. A friend of mine borrowed my car last week. He must have used the handle for something and left it there."

"Did you laugh when you found it?"

"Laugh? Are you serious? I was furious."

Flying Eagle roared with laughter again and slapped me on the back. "It's a good thing you came back this summer, Screaming Hawk. You've got a lot to learn about the ways of the Spirit."

He stood up. "Let's go back. I'll help you unload your car. Unless the Spirit causes it to start raining again," he added with a laugh. "In that case, Screaming Hawk, you are on your own."

❧ 2 ❧

I was tired from the two days of hard driving and my ordeal with the flat tire. After Flying Eagle helped me unload the contents of the car into my small but adequate room, I unpacked my suitcase and took a nap. Shortly before dinner time I went to meet Flying Eagle at his lodge.

"You look more rested," said Flying Eagle as I came through the door.

"I am."

"Good. I hope you are hungry. Running Deer is cooking tonight. As you know, she is the best cook in the village.

"Last summer you were lucky; Buffalo Woman was away visiting relatives. But she hasn't left yet on her visit this summer and it was her turn to cook again last week. Her cooking is terrible. I and the rest of the village nearly starved to death. But everyone will be there tonight looking for a good meal from Running Deer. They will be glad to see you."

As we entered the dining hall, various people spoke to me. I spent the next minutes greeting those already waiting there and others as they arrived for the long awaited meal. I was warmly welcomed by all. It felt good to be in their midst again.

Finally, Running Deer and her assistant brought the first of what proved to be a series of steaming hot trays out of the kitchen. There was a loud rumble as all who were seated simultaneously pushed their chairs back from the tables and started a marginally controlled stampede to the serving line. I struggled to keep up with Flying Eagle as he scrambled across the room. Despite his age he managed to arrive in time for a coveted position somewhere in the front third of the line. He smiled and chuckled to himself, obviously proud of his accomplishment.

"When the village met a few years ago and decided to build this dining hall I thought it was a good idea," he said. "Some of our elderly people, who were living alone, were not caring well for themselves and the younger ones who were single were finding it lonely to eat most of their meals alone. It gave us a place to gather and enjoy being together. Even some of the families have chosen to come here regularly for meals. But every time it is Buffalo

Woman's turn to cook I have to rethink the wisdom of our decision. In the midst of a gastronomic crisis it is hard to remember the years of joy, satisfaction and nourishment that I have received here."

He glanced around the room.

"Look at these people!" he said with mock seriousness. "You would think they hadn't eaten for a week.

"You know, it's amazing how many people in the village decide to abstain from food as a spiritual discipline each time it's Buffalo Woman's turn to cook. She has done more to advance the spirituality of the people than I have.

"Her husband died some years ago. There has been a rumor in the village that the cause of his death was indigestion."

He continued to ramble on for another couple of minutes entertaining himself with various comments that he mumbled into my ear about Buffalo Woman's cooking. I felt uncomfortable. I had never seen him in a mood like that before. Although some of his comments were amusing, I didn't like listening to him denigrate one of the women of the village.

"You don't seem to like Buffalo Woman," I said, stating the obvious.

His smile vanished instantly. "Well, enough of that," he said. "It is so good to have you here," he said, giving me a quick squeeze around the shoulders with one arm.

We finally reached the food. Flying Eagle helped himself to large portions. We carried our plates to a nearby table and sat down.

He continued. "In your letter you said that you are teaching religion at a college now. How do you like it?"

"The students are wonderful but my colleague in the department is kind of a pain. He is extremely conservative. Everything is either black or white to him. Since I don't think anything is black or white, we argue frequently. Sometimes it's hard to believe that we are talking about the same religion. I would like to get your thoughts about it when we get a chance."

"Good," he said, nodding his head. "We will talk about it later."

"How are you doing?" I asked.

"Not bad. Things have been going well in the village. I have been in good health."

The expression in his eyes suddenly changed to one that I can only describe as a puzzling mixture of pleasure and irritation.

"I had another conversation with Star Man a few days ago. He talked about you."

I felt excited. "Oh? What did he say?"

"I will to tell you about it when we have time," he said flatly.

I was intensely curious about what Star Man had said but it was obvious that I would have to wait. We talked on for a while about various things. As we consumed our second helpings, he brought me up to date on what had been happening with some of the people in the village over the past months and I gave him more information about what I had been doing since I had last seen him.

We both left the dining hall over-stuffed but happy and waddled back to Flying Eagle's lodge for more informal conversation. We talked and joked like school boys. Finally, I said good night, returned to my room and fell asleep almost immediately.

❦ 3 ❦

I met Flying Eagle the next morning for breakfast. After the meal we headed into the forest for a long walk and deep conversation.

"Last night," Flying Eagle began, "you said that you are in frequent conflict with the other professor of religion where you teach. We will begin there with your instruction today.

"You said," he continued, "that it is hard to believe the two of you are dealing with the same religion. I believe you have already gotten close to the heart of the problem. The body of information both of you are dealing with is the same but you have radically different approaches to it. The difference between your approach and his is so great that it really is almost like dealing with two different religions. Christianity and all the major religions I know anything about all contain two major approaches. The first sees the Spirit as being primarily concerned with one's thoughts and conduct. In that approach there is much focus on doctrine, rules and structure. The doctrine can be learned and one is expected to believe it. The rules of conduct too can be learned and great emphasis is placed upon following them. The truth is seen as being contained within a certain body of information. One is expected to train one's mind to accept that body of information, to think proper thoughts and to have proper conduct.

"The other approach deals primarily with the impact of the Spirit upon one's heart. It is a more mystical approach. There is much mystery and little that is absolute. Rules and doctrine are viewed as sometimes being useful but are always inadequate and incomplete. The encounter itself with the Spirit is seen as the essence of religion, and truth is thought to be something that can be experienced but can never be explained adequately or comprehended fully. In that view, doctrine is only a pointer toward the truth rather than being the truth itself.

"Your colleague seems to have the former approach and you the latter. The two of you will rarely agree. The rules and doctrine that bring life and meaning to him bring a sense of restriction and death to you. It is that way and no amount of discussion will change it. The important thing to remember is that you are not there to change him. The Spirit, in time, will show him another approach but it may not be during his present life time. If the change of approach were forced upon him too soon it would prevent him from growing properly. The first approach comes at an earlier stage of spiritual development for a person but it is a stage that is very important to experience. During that stage, some awareness of the Spirit emerges and intellectual certainty of the Spirit's reality develops. If that stage does not occur, a person can not make the transition later into the realm of understanding the Spirit in a less restrictive way. The first approach limits the Spirit to something that can be comprehended. The second approach allows the Spirit to be something that can not be comprehended. Do not force your colleague to see religion in the way that you do. He must experience the Spirit the first way before he can ever experience the Spirit the second way. Allow him to be the way he is."

"While we are on this subject," I said, "there is something that I have wondered about for years. Some of my friends are agnostics and one or two are atheists. I feel far more harmony with them when we are talking about our obvious differences of religious beliefs than I do when I am talking to people who approach religion the way my colleague in the religion department does. Why is that? Logically I would expect to have less in common with an atheist."

"I am pleased that you can sense that harmony even though your mind is confused by it. You are sensitive to your heart.

"The reason you feel the harmony is because many agnostics and atheists are at a higher stage of spiritual development than those who follow a traditional religion of clear-cut rules and beliefs, like your colleague.

"Although there are many ways to talk about this, I think it is helpful to identify four basic stages of spiritual growth. In the First Stage, people are almost totally self-serving and have little or no interest in the ways of the Spirit. They do not love others and they recognize no value that is higher than meeting their own needs. I call that stage Self-Centered Spirituality. As they progress they may become "converted" and move into the Second Stage which I call Traditional Spirituality. That stage is characterized by clear cut rules and beliefs, like those of your colleague at the college. Most people who are active in churches are in that second stage. The Third Stage, Skeptical Spirituality, is one of questioning traditional religious views and values. Your agnostic and atheistic friends are probably in that category. Beyond that is the Fourth Stage, Mystical Spirituality. In that stage the Spirit is experienced in the mystery of that which can be encountered but cannot be explained. You and all other mystics are in that Fourth Stage.

"The progression through the stages is not always clear-cut. Some people may experience two of the stages at the same time for a while, such as the person who has serious doubts about some things but does not totally reject all traditional religious teachings. Others may bounce back and forth between two stages for a time.

"It is important to understand that there can also be significant differences between people within the same stage. A highly advanced Stage Two person will see and understand things quite differently from a beginning Stage Two person.

"Most traditional, Stage Two, religious people do not understand that as people progress on their spiritual journeys they must pass through a stage of skepticism before they can experience the Spirit the way mystics do. They may fear that they are losing their faith if they develop doubts or start questioning the true nature of the Spirit. People in Stage Two tend to look down on those who have those doubts, calling them terms such as 'back sliders' or 'non-believers.' They do not understand that the period of skepticism is, in fact, a time of reorganizing one's religious understanding and leaving behind views that stand in the way of experiencing the mystery of the Spirit.

"The reason you feel some harmony with your skeptical friends is because they are only one stage removed from where you are. Although you do not agree about many things, you can still understand each other. It is very difficult to communicate effectively with someone who is two stages away, such as your colleague. The views of a Stage Four Mystic are often threatening to a Stage Two person with a traditional approach to religion. And many of the less developed mystics, those who are not yet securely rooted in Stage Four, feel threatened by the Stage Two approach because for them to return to Stage Two thinking would be a regression. Violent conflict has emerged at times between those in different stages, the most notable of which was the practice of Stage Two Christians burning mystics at the stake in the name of religion.

"But I have said enough for today. Let's enjoy the beauty of the forest."

We walked on in silence.

✤ 4 ✤

The next day we returned to the forest. After we had been walking for perhaps twenty minutes, Flying Eagle said, "Let's stop here and sit for a while." He pointed to a pleasant area under one of the large trees near the trail. "I want to talk to you."

When we were comfortably settled he said, "Last summer I taught you about how to be a warrior. But to be truly effective the warrior must continue his spiritual growth. Therefore, this summer we will focus on your spritual growth.

"I told you that Star Man came to me again a few days ago. I will tell you about that now."

Again I felt a twinge of excitement. My mind flashed back to my only meeting with Star Man nearly a year earlier, and I relived the power of that event. He had come to me late in the night as I waited for him alone by the fire. He wore Indian buckskins and had a single silver eagle's feather in his head band. I remembered his teachings about love, but, most of all, I remembered that soul shattering moment at the end of his visit when, as we parted, he raised his arm and I saw the wound in his hand. It was then that I had recognized him as Jesus.

Flying Eagle continued, "He came to me in the forest nine days ago and spoke to me. He said that you would be coming soon and that I must teach you about The Principle Paths to Divine Circumstance now; that I must not wait until later. I argued with him about it. I told him that you were not ready. I said that I had not been told about all of The Principal Paths until I had been under instruction for several years and that it was dangerous to learn too much too soon. He said that he knew all about my training and that he also knew all about yours and that he didn't need any bullheaded medicine man telling him how to run the Universe or instructing him about when to share knowledge with a student.

"What could I say? He outranks me," Flying Eagle said with a sheepish little grin. "Sometimes I think he is misinformed and that I know more about how to run a good Universe than he does, but I have to admit that every time

I have obeyed his orders things have worked out rather well. I have to give him credit. And so far I have never won an argument with him.

"So, I have my orders. I am to teach you about The Principle Paths to Divine Circumstance now. Now! Not when I think you are ready, but now! Who does he think he is, telling me how to run my training program?" He sputtered on in mock rage for another few minutes obviously enjoying his own monologue about how Star Man never fully appreciates the wisdom of his own medicine men and how difficult he is to work for and how he has never arranged for his employees to be paid what they are really worth.

In the midst of a threat directed upward, that he was going to organize a medicine man's union and tackle the problems with management once and for all, Flying Eagle suddenly stopped, looked at me and said, "You know, I ought to be on stage. I'm really good at this!"

We laughed together. Then he became serious and said, "It is dangerous to learn about The Paths. If you misunderstand these teachings, or you apply them at the wrong times or in the wrong ways, you can do great harm to yourself and others. The Universe did not come into being to be manipulated like a toy for our own amusement. It is quite possible to manipulate physical matter and to make it do whatever you want but that must not be done without purpose. Some learn The Paths and then use them to gain riches or fame or to control others. You must never use this knowledge for that purpose. If you do, it will eventually turn on you and you may die lonely and bitter amongst all the things that you have manipulated out of life.

"The true medicine man has the power to do many things but chooses to do only that which is helpful to others and expresses the will of the Spirit. If you always follow that principle you will do no harm. But that is not as easy as it sounds. We all have ways of convincing ourselves that the Spirit wants what we want; it's our way of avoiding true servanthood. The Spirit wants each of us to be free to give of ourselves to others. When we do that without seeking to get rewarded for our good behavior, tremendous power is generated, power that can be channeled in many useful directions. When we do something for selfish gain, or in order to look good in the eyes of others, the power generated is self-serving. It may make us look good in the eyes of others but it is not available to bring about the deeper will of the Spirit. You must be careful. You must act out of pure motives or you will decrease your power to give and decrease your power to bring about the will of the Spirit."

He paused and looked at me long and hard.

"I have warned you. Are you sure you want me to continue with this teaching?"

"Yes," I said.

"I knew you would say that," he said, as he looked at the ground with a sad expression on his face. Then he took a deep breath and continued. "I will follow Star Man's instructions. I will teach you.

"Events in a person's life do not unfold by random, nor do they unfold according to rigid laws that can not be changed. Most events unfold according to a principle known as Divine Circumstance. When you follow The Paths your awareness of Divine Circumstance in your life will increase dramatically. You will see the Spirit working powerfully in everything that happens to you. But it is important to follow The Paths in the proper order. Some follow The Paths but deliberately alter the order of them because they are seeking to bring about their own will rather than the will of the Spirit. When you follow The Paths in the proper order, your will and the Spirit's will will merge. Then you will discover the Spirit in all that is and all that happens.

"The first great principle, and the one that must always be applied first, is to seek the will of the Spirit in the largest context. This is called The Path of the Greatest Good. If one seeks the will of the Spirit only within a small context, the Spirit's will may be different than it is when one seeks the Spirit's will in the largest context. The greatest good rather than a lesser good must be sought. This principle is frequently violated by those who are early on the path of spiritual development. People who are spiritually immature will quite frequently seek the will of the Spirit only within the small context of their own desires. Within that context, there are certain things that the Spirit wills that are not in keeping with the will of the Spirit in the larger context of the Greatest Good. For example, people may pray for a pay raise because they want or need more money. In the narrow context of a person's immediate situation, the Spirit may agree that he or she needs more money and the Spirit may cause that to come about. But in the larger context, the context of the Greatest Good, it may be the will of the Spirit for that person to change jobs and pursue a career that will be of greater service to others. Making more money in the present job may be good but it might not lead to fulfilling the greater will of the Spirit. The Spirit usually responds to us within the context that we allow. The Spirit does not force us to operate within the context of the Greatest Good. We must choose it. When we do choose it, there is the potential of great power for change being released.

"When Star Man was on earth as Jesus, he was following The Path of the Greatest Good when he prayed, 'not my will but yours be done,' on the night before he was crucified. In the smaller context of his own safety, he could have prayed to escape those who were seeking his destruction and the Spirit would have responded. But The Path of the Greatest Good led him to the cross. It takes courage to follow The Path of the Greatest Good because sometimes it leads to great personal sacrifice.

"The Spirit allows us to choose the context within which we will operate. When we follow The Path of the Greatest Good we deliberately, courageously, choose the largest context for good.

"But merely pursuing The Greatest Good with our actions is not enough, Screaming Hawk. The Spirit desires that our actions be aligned with our wills. When we pursue the second Path, The Path of the Inner Journey, we discover that much of the time we do not will The Greatest Good. The Inner Journey is an exploration of our own inner issues and needs, and the evil that lies within us. As we follow that Path we discover that we have a natural tendency to seek a lessor, self-serving good. We discover that our personal will and the Spirit's will are in conflict much of the time.

"People try to deal with that conflict in various ways. Some try to avoid the conflict by ignoring their own will. They try to act in accordance with the Spirit's will, even though they are not truly seeking the Greatest Good. Others try to make deals with the Spirit in an attempt to change the Spirit's will to conform to their own. They may promise to do certain things if the Spirit will answer a particular prayer. And some people project their own will onto their sense of the Spirit's will. When that happens, they may truly believe that they are following the will of the Spirit when, in reality, they are only following their own desire for a lessor good."

"But, Flying Eagle, aren't the Spirit's will and our own will the same sometimes?"

"Yes, and that kind of alignment of one's own will with the Spirit's will can produce great power. Sometimes that alignment does occur naturally. By seriously following The Inner Journey one will be able to recognize when the two wills are in alignment. At other times one may have to make a conscious choice to will what the Spirit wills. Contrary to what some have said, the true spiritual journey does not cause one to lose awareness of one's own will in the Spirit's will. It does not lead to fusion with the Spirit; it leads to union with the Spirit. Just as those in a healthy marriage each maintain an awareness of their own will, even when their will happens to be in alignment with the will of their spouse, so it is when one lives in relationship with the Spirit. Coming into union with the Spirit does not result in losing one's own will; the union leads to the discovery that sometimes one naturally wills what the Spirit wills and at other times one must choose what the Spirit wills. But be careful about giving up your will to the Spirit without making a conscious choice. That is unhealthy. One must choose out of a true inner desire to will what the Spirit wills.

"There is much more to teach you about The Paths but that is enough for today. Too much instruction in one day can make one lose one's sense of humor. You must be able to make the Spirit laugh."

On that strange note the session ended. We walked back to the village in silence.

❧ 5 ❧

The next day we returned to the forest for the teaching session. As soon as we sat down I asked Flying Eagle my question.

"Flying Eagle, yesterday you said that I must be able to make the Spirit laugh. What did you mean?"

"You are getting ahead of yourself, Screaming Hawk. That is contained in the fourth of The Principle Paths to Divine Circumstance. We are not there yet. The order is very important."

"O.K., I'll wait. Can you tell me about The Third Path now?"

"Yes." That was all he said. We sat in silence for perhaps thirty minutes. It was deep silence, meditative silence, silence where no words were spoken and where none were needed.

Finally he said, "The third principle is The Path of Silence. It is very important but it is often neglected in your culture. Christians are always talking to God. Talk, talk, talk. They go to church and they talk. They talk, but they do not listen. Some of them say prayers at home. There, too, they talk without listening. Some act as if God has nothing to say, that he is mute. That is not the case; the Spirit talks to those who listen in silence.

"Silence is important, far more important than most Christians realize. It is in the silence that the Spirit speaks most clearly. It is when one is inactive that the Spirit is most active. Mystics know that. But most Christians today act as if they never heard that. Follow The Path of Silence.

"The fourth principle is The Way of Humor. For some reason your religion teaches very little about this. It is very important. To have great power one must have a sense of humor and must share it with the Spirit. Most people assume that the Spirit is serious all the time. That is not the case. The Spirit has a wonderful sense of humor and enjoys a good laugh. If you want to draw close to the Spirit, you must learn how to make the Spirit laugh and you yourself must learn how to laugh with the Spirit. When the Spirit tells you a joke, you need to be free to laugh and enjoy it."

"Now wait a minute. You mean to tell me that the Spirit tells you jokes?"

"Sometimes. But the Spirit is also a practical joker. The Spirit causes things to happen that are funny."

"You're putting me on."

"No. I am speaking the truth. In order to enter into a deep relationship with the Spirit you must understand that the Spirit has a sense of humor. One of your problems, Screaming Hawk, is that you take life so seriously all the time. Sometimes life is serious; sometimes it is not. When it is not serious you still think that it is and you act like it is. You have the same problem with the Spirit. The Spirit is not serious all the time but you act as though he is."

"I don't understand."

"I know you don't understand! I told Star Man that you would not understand. He agreed that you would not understand but he said that it was my job to make you understand. He said that you were ready to learn The Fourth Path now, that you needed to learn it now and that it was my job to teach you. Now you tell me, how do you teach somebody who does not have a sense of humor about life, that the Spirit does have a sense of humor? It can't be done. It's impossible. How did I get this job anyway?

"You know, if Star Man didn't like you so much I wouldn't waste my time on you. He thinks you have potential. Sometimes I wonder about that. To be honest, sometimes I wonder about Star Man. I mean, you have to wonder about anybody who would hire Judas Iscariot to work for him. It's no wonder things turned out badly for him. I told Star Man that the next time he decides to save the world he should call me in to handle the staffing interviews for him."

"You said that to Star Man?" I asked in disbelief.

"Yes."

"What did he say?"

"He laughed."

"He laughed?"

"Yes. He laughed. That surprises you, doesn't it? He laughs a lot when I talk to him. He has a good sense of humor. Most people don't know that but he does. And until you realize that, you will not be able to understand him or some of his actions."

"But if that's true, why hasn't somebody told me that before now?"

"Because that knowledge is dangerous."

"Dangerous? How can it be dangerous?"

"That knowledge must be handled with great care. It can open the way to a deeper relationship with the Spirit or to putting oneself above the Spirit. Some move from laughing with the Spirit to laughing at the Spirit. There is a great difference between the two. Those who laugh with the Spirit find great joy and freedom. Those who laugh at the Spirit put themselves above the Spirit. To put oneself above the Spirit can lead one back to worshiping oneself as the God of one's own universe."

"But weren't you laughing at the Spirit when you made those comments about his poor judgement in hiring Judas?"

"No. I was laughing with the Spirit. I was really laughing with him about the irony of his using his knowledge to choose the path of destruction. He laughed with me about it. But as you have just pointed out, the difference can be quite subtle sometimes. That is why it is so important to follow The Path of the Inner Journey before undertaking The Path of Humor. One must know oneself rather well or one can slip into laughing at the Spirit without even realizing it.

"But that's enough for today. There is much more to teach you but you need to absorb what I have already told you first. And by the way, don't look so serious. I have never seen anybody look so serious about humor."

He stood up abruptly and headed back down the trail to the village muttering loudly to himself as he went.

"I told Star Man that it was impossible. Did he listen to me? No. Does he ever listen to me when I tell him how to run the universe? How did I get this job anyway? Who does he think he is? 'Now!' Star Man said, 'Now!' Can you believe that? He wants me to teach Screaming Hawk about humor now. Hopeless. Utterly hopeless. I couldn't make him understand...."

He was still muttering but I could no longer make out most of the words as he moved farther down the trail. Then he stopped, turned in my direction and shouted, "Hopeless!" one more time. He paused and looked up indicating that his last comment was intended not just for my hearing but also for The One Who Speaks in the Silence. Then he turned abruptly and continued down the trail. Peace returned to the forest and I was left alone with my solemn, humorless thoughts.

༄ 6 ༄

I thought, meditated, wrote in my journal, and prayed for days about divine humor. It did not make sense to me. I could not, despite what Flying Eagle had told me, imagine God cracking jokes. It was contrary to my whole concept of The Divine. I could not imagine God's laughing. Humor is a human trait, only a human trait. Or is it? Surely I was not implying that God was not capable of laughing. It was rather presumptuous on my part to think that God was incapable of doing something that people quite regularly do. And yet, I could not imagine God's telling a joke or playing a practical joke. Why not? Well, because God wouldn't want to tell a joke. Why not? Because God is too dignified for that sort of thing. Was I sure of that? Well, no, I was not sure of that. Then it occurred to me what the real problem was. I think of a person's humor as an expression of their own personality. Since God doesn't have a personality, I mused, he doesn't have a sense of humor. But what if God really does have a personality? Could it be that having a personal relationship with God would include getting to know his personality? I had never thought of it that way. I believed that it was possible to have a personal relationship with God but somehow it had always seemed like a one way relationship. God's relating to my personality. God's knowing me. God's telling things to me. Could it really be a two way relationship where he interacts with my personality and I interact with his?

One day, as Flying Eagle and I were taking a long walk together, I told him about my recent thoughts regarding the possibility that God does have a personality.

Flying Eagle stopped walking and turned facing me.

"You surprise me, Screaming Hawk. Of course God has a personality. Don't you see yet what you have done? You created a god who does not have a personality; then you established a relationship with that god with no personality, and you became intimate with that god with no personality. Then you tried to figure out the god that you created.

"But you don't see it that way, do you?"

"No, Flying Eagle. What do you mean I created a god?"

"That's exactly what you did. Knowing God, knowing the Spirit, knowing Star Man, is just that, knowing him. *You* don't know *him*. You know about him and you call that knowing him. It is not the same. *Your* relationship is with an idea, not with God. God is not an idea. You created a god who matches your ideas about God. You did that and you still don't see the folly of it. That's what is so amazing about you. Your mind works and you keep thinking about having a relationship with God. Then you act as if thinking about it is the same as having the relationship. It is not. You think about God far more than you experience God. Give up thinking about God. You will never develop a relationship with God through your thoughts; your thoughts can only lead you to a relationship with the god you created."

"Wait a minute! Flying Eagle, are you telling me that all this time I have been relating to my own idea of God instead of God himself?"

"That's exactly what I am telling you. God is not the way you think he is. God is the way he is."

"I don't understand."

"There you go again. Of course you don't understand. You think you are supposed to understand God. The only god you are ever going to understand is the god that you, yourself, have created. That god you can understand. But you do not encounter God himself with your understanding. That's why the issue of God's humor is so important. The god you created has no humor; so you think God has no humor. That's the way most people operate. They create their own god and call it God. Then they relate to the idea of the god they have created and call it a relationship with God. That is what you have been doing. Do you understand now?"

"Yes. But I don't like what I am hearing."

"Of course you don't. Nobody likes to hear that they have been relating to their own creation and calling it God. But until you make that discovery your god will always be limited to your own power and you will never be able to truly experience The Circumstances."

"What do The Circumstances have to do with this Flying Eagle?"

"The Circumstances have everything to do with this. It is through The Circumstances that the true God works. Your god works through making what you want to happen happen. The true God works through circumstances most of the time."

"I don't understand."

"I know," he said and walked away.

🌿 7 🌿

The more I thought, the more confused I became. All I seemed to be really clear about was that Flying Eagle was telling me that I did not really know God and that I had been worshiping a god of my own creation. That was disturbing, really disturbing. I needed to talk more about it. I went looking for Flying Eagle and found him in his room, lying on the bed reading a mystery novel.

"Can I come in?" I asked, not wanting to interrupt, but wanting to interrupt.

"Yes," he said putting the book down. "I have been waiting for you. I knew you were coming."

"How did you know that?"

"Because I was just getting to the good part," he said, making a slight gesture in the direction of the book. "People always show up with deep and probing theological questions when I get into the really good parts of a novel. It is a little trick the Spirit has been playing on me for years. He enjoys it; so I tolerate it. It does no good to complain. Every time I complain about it he chuckles and tells me that it builds character.

"But I have my own ways of getting back at him. I like to work crossword puzzles in my head during the ceremonies. Not in the really important parts mind you, just in the parts that people think are important. Everybody gets really quiet and solemn, and there I am working crossword puzzles in my head. He has threatened to fire me over it a number of times but every time he does, I remind him that he can't afford to fire me. I tell him that if he does, I will tell all and let the people know that the really solemn parts of the rituals are not very important. He knows that the people really like those parts and that it is those parts that keep many of the people coming back year after year. I tell him that after my unwarranted termination I will see to it that only truly committed people show up for the ceremonies. He knows as well as I do that he wouldn't have much of a crowd to work with then. We laugh about it and then he lets me off with a threat. I've been doing crossword puzzles in my head for years and we have been making threats and counter threats for years but we still keep working together.

"But you did not come to hear about that."

"Well I'm not so sure, Flying Eagle, maybe that's exactly the kind of thing I need to hear about. I think you are right about my having created my own god, one without a sense of humor."

"There is hope for you, Screaming Hawk!" he said. Then with a light hearted chuckle he added, "Not much hope, mind you, but a little hope."

"It bothers me," I continued, "that I may have been worshiping a self-created god all these years without realizing it."

"I can understand that it might bother you," he said. "Interestingly enough, people who make that discovery usually make it at exactly the point you are making it, when they come up against The Way of Humor and realize that their god does not have a sense of humor. It is at that point that many of them get serious about discovering what God is really like. There is a danger though. Some leave the Path at this point and choose to continue to worship their own god, as opposed to worshiping the true God of the Universe. At each point along the spiritual journey there are dangers and there are some who succumb to them. You are facing one of those dangers now. In order to move on, you will have to face the fact that you have been wrong all those years about God, that you were not worshiping him in spirit and in truth."

"That's not a pleasant thought."

"No, it is not. And you will have to deal with your own pride in order to admit that you were wrong about something as important as that. All of us like to think that we are right and we even tend to create a god who will tell us we are right. That is the irony of it all. It is only when we are willing to be wrong about everything that we have the capability of becoming right about what is most important, the true nature of God."

"Did you ever go through this, Flying Eagle? Did you ever discover that you had been worshiping a false god?"

"Oh yes. It was the most embarrassing period of my whole life. I was already a practicing medicine man when I discovered it. Star Man came to me and started telling me jokes. I thought I was going crazy. Then he told me about The Way of Humor. Like you, it led me to the realization that I had not truly known God. Like you, I had created a humorless god and had been worshiping that god. Without realizing it, I had even been teaching people things about god that were not true.

"I was in agony for weeks. I tried to resign. I told Star Man that I had been a fraud without knowing it and that I could no longer be a medicine man of honor. He laughed and said that always happens, just at the point when someone starts to become really useful he wants to quit. He refused to accept my resignation. I tried to quit ten times. He kept laughing at me saying that I was missing the point, that until I realized I had been a fool I could never work effectively with his people.

"I didn't like the sound of that. Somehow being a fool did not seem like appropriate credentials to pursue my noble profession. But he convinced me. He said that as long as I needed to be right I could never explore the mysteries of the Spirit in depth. Later, I came to understand what he meant. When one enters into the deeper levels of the mystery, truth can only be experienced; it can not be understood or explained. To know truths that can neither be understood nor put into words makes one appear to be a fool. Out of the experience of the unexplainable one comes to deal with reality in ways that do not make sense to others. One does things that are strange; one says things that are strange; one no longer fits into society."

He paused a moment and waved his right hand in a small circle in the air as he made a fist.

"What time is it?" he asked.

I glanced at my wrist. My watch was gone. I knew I had been wearing it; I had looked at it to check the time just before I entered the room. I looked back at Flying Eagle.

"Are you looking for this?" he said, opening his fist.

I couldn't believe my eyes. He was holding my watch. I had not come within an arm's reach of him at any point and yet he was holding my watch.

"That's fantastic!" I sputtered. "How did you do that?"

"I can not tell you," he said.

"Please tell me. I really want to know."

"You do not understand. I cannot tell you. I do not understand it myself. I cannot explain it. I can make it happen but it is as big a mystery to me as it is to you."

"Can you do other things like that?"

"Yes, many things. But they are all unimportant.

"I want you to understand something, Screaming Hawk. I don't like doing those things when other people are around. The only reason I did it in front of you was because I needed to show you what I was talking about.

"You might think it is nice to be able to astound people in that way. It is not. I feel like a fool when I do those things. I do not understand and I can not explain to others how I do them. All I know is that I experience reality in a different way than most other people do and because of that I can do those things. But it is not altogether pleasant to live in a different relationship to reality from most other people. When I am at a gathering of other medicine men, I belong. But when I am with most other people, I do not belong. I do not share their understanding of reality and I do not experience life in the way they do. It is painful to be constantly among people with whom one does not belong.

"But back to my point. I am a fool. I can do things that I do not understand. That causes me pain but I am no longer afraid of being a fool.

"You are a fool also, Screaming Hawk. You have discovered that you were worshiping a god that you yourself created. That makes you a fool. Although it is not pleasant, accepting that one is a fool opens the way for a deeper relationship with the Spirit because one is open to experiencing that which one cannot understand.

"God has a sense of humor. You did not know that before. Now you do.

"You are a fool. You did not know that before either. Now you do.

"Now get out of here and let me get back to my novel!"

I really thought he was angry for a moment. Then he smiled and winked at me as he handed me my watch. I turned and left his room, closing the door behind me.

I paused in the hallway for a moment, regaining my composure. Through the closed door I couldn't help hearing him muttering to the unseen Spirit.

"Always at the best part! You got me again!

"But just you wait! You think the crossword puzzles are obnoxious? You haven't seen anything yet!"

❧ 8 ❧

The issue of divine humor continued to intrigue me. It seemed to be opening the way for a new understanding of God and his actions. I thought about how often in human relationships serious misunderstandings develop when one person takes a statement seriously that another has meant as a joke. Discovering that a statement was made in jest can instantly change one's perception of the meaning of the statement and one's perceptions of the character of the one making the comment as well. Could the same be true of one's relationship with God? Are there times when we fail to recognize divine humor and misunderstand both the message and the character of God as a result? What if life is not as serious as I had supposed? What if there is an element of humor in the way that life unfolds for us, an element that we often fail to recognize?

I thought about Shakespeare's *A Comedy of Errors*, a play about a long series of complications and misunderstandings. Life seems that way for all of us at times. But when we encounter a series of problems, do we realize that it is a comedy? Was my ordeal in the rain with that flat tire really a divine comedy? When I had been in that sort of situation in the past I had not even cracked a smile.

I had heard various people who have endured calamities state the importance of having a sense of humor. I had thought of those people as imposing humor on a humorless set of circumstances as a device to make it all more bearable for them. But could it be that, rather than imposing humor where there was none, they had simply discovered the divine humor that actually was there?

I had tended to think of all calamities as bad. Physical destruction and the loss of one's property were serious. Were they serious to me partly because I took physical possessions so seriously? If our having lots of physical possessions is not important to God, as the Bible so often proclaims, and if our over-valuing physical possessions does prevent us from being in touch with higher values, perhaps God does not take calamities involving physical destruction as seriously as we do. Perhaps they are not a cruel act of nature.

Could they, at times, be a playful reminder that our physical possessions really are not as important as we think they are? Is it possible to see a calamity as an expression of divine humor? Is it truly possible to laugh with God over the loss of things that are not valuable beyond the value we place on them? Could God be revealing an intimate side of his personality, his sense of humor, in the midst of calamities?

I was confused and troubled. I did not like the image of God laughing in the midst of a hurricane while people were losing their possessions. And there was one more thing that I found deeply troubling. What about the loss of life that occurs in the midst of some calamities; does God laugh at that too?

In my next session with Flying Eagle I told him what I had been thinking and reviewed for him my troubling questions about God's sense of humor.

"You are starting to delve into the deeper questions about the nature of God," he said. "You will not resolve those questions with your mind. You must first resolve them with your heart. Only when you can feel the humor of God can you understand the humor of God."

Somehow Flying Eagle's response was not very satisfying.

"But can't you tell me something that would be helpful in the mean time?"

"Yes. It is impossible for you, Screaming Hawk, to experience God's humor."

"Thanks a lot! And that's supposed to make me feel better?"

"You did not ask for something to make you feel better. You asked for something that would be helpful. The two are not the same."

"O.K., O.K., then don't tell me something that will be helpful; tell me something that will make me feel better."

"You will learn to laugh with God."

"Now wait a minute. You just told me that it was impossible for me to experience God's humor and now you are telling me that I will learn to laugh with God. Which is true?"

"Both are true."

Needless to say, I was even more confused than before. I pressed on.

"What do you mean both are true? How can both be true?"

"Your problem is that you don't understand the difference between what is impossible and what will not happen. It is impossible for you to experience God's humor, but that does not mean that it will not happen. Many things that are impossible do happen. Surely you know that.

"It was impossible for me to take your watch off your wrist without touching you; wasn't it?"

"Yes."

"It still happened; did it not?

"Yes."

"That which was impossible happened.

"When something is impossible, it can not happen within the present system. Within your system, it was not possible for me to take your watch, but, as I told you, I do not experience reality in the same way that most others do. My experience of reality is not the same as yours. Within my system, objects can be moved by one's will. Within your system, objects can be moved only through touching them or by applying some other kind of force to them. What is impossible in your system can still happen in mine.

"Within your system it is not possible for you to experience God's humor. But if you were in a different system, you could experience God's humor.

"So, Screaming Hawk, get out of your system and let it happen."

"But what system am I in now and what other system do I need to be in?"

"I have already told you. You are in the system of your mind. You need to be in the system of your heart. In the system of your heart, things can happen that are impossible in the system of your mind."

"How do I change systems?"

"It is easy, but it is also difficult. I will tell you this much today, it is easier to make the transition when you are confused."

Having said that, he held up his hand indicating that I was not to ask any more questions now. The session was over.

❧ 9 ❧

I felt no closer to experiencing God's humor than I had before, but Flying Eagle's teaching about that which is impossible in one system being possible in another intrigued me. That must be what a miracle is, reality being encountered from a different system than the one the observer normally operates within. I realized that many things, like television or flying in airplanes, that we consider normal would have seemed miraculous to anyone a hundred years ago. Our perception of reality is different now and our expectations are different.

But I was still troubled by the concept of God as a practical joker. When Flying Eagle met me for our next session I asked him about it.

"I was wondering when you were going to ask me for more information about that," he said. "I could tell that it was troubling you."

"Somehow God as a practical joker seems cruel, uncaring, impersonal - all the things that I have been taught that God is not."

"That is because you do not yet know how to laugh with God.

"I will tell you something now that will not help you to experience God's humor but it will help you to understand God's humor. As your teacher, I am here, in part, to help you learn and understand. Understanding is useful but it does not take the place of experience." He paused a moment as if for emphasis and then said, "You are the subject of God's humor when he is playing a practical joke. God is being extremely intimate when he encounters you in this way. But in order to laugh with God at his practical jokes you must understand yourself. The joke is about you. The joke is to make you look at yourself or your behavior, to look and to understand. The humor depends upon your understanding yourself. If you do not understand yourself, God's actions may, at times, seem cruel and impersonal. But his practical jokes are intensely personal and to understand them you must know yourself. That is why it is so important to follow the Path of the Inner Journey before you try to follow the Path of Humor."

"But does a person ever understand himself fully?"

"No, not in this lifetime. But the more one understands himself, the more one can experience God's humor and learn to laugh with God.

"Perhaps an example of what I am talking about would be helpful.

"Many people consider money to be important, far more important than it is. They measure success by how much money they have or how much they are earning and they make many of their decisions based on money. Those people are often subject to God's practical jokes but they rarely understand the humor. People who overvalue money are frequently subject to financial reversals or tax problems or investments that go sour. In those events, God is showing them that they are basing their security and happiness on money. When their money becomes threatened, or in short supply, they become insecure and unhappy. Because of that, God often arranges events in such a way that they will experience that discomfort. A crash in the stock market is an opportunity for many people to look at themselves and the discomfort they feel, and an opportunity to laugh at the ridiculousness of basing their lives on little figures that are produced as a result of people using hand signals and shouting back and forth at each other in some distant city. Now that is pretty ridiculous, don't you agree?"

"Well yes, but I don't think it is very funny to see a person's life savings slip away because those numbers are getting smaller and smaller."

"But that is because you think that money is important and that it can buy security and happiness for people. Except for brief periods, there is little relationship between the size of the numbers and a person's sense of security or happiness. Those who understand that are able to laugh at themselves when they see themselves getting upset about the numbers. I realize that this may seem uncaring of God but it is not. The Spirit's greatest concern is that people grow, develop and mature. Many people's growth is hampered by their riches. When the Spirit takes away that which is hampering a person's growth, it is a loving act. To those who are too attached to their riches it is seen as a cruel act. But those who know themselves to be overly attached to money have the capability of laughing at the loss and knowing that the joke is on them. You see, the numbers merely go up or they go down. We are the ones who assign value to the numbers and decide that having more is better than having less. But in the realm of the Spirit having more is not necessarily better, in fact having less is usually better. The Spirit knows that. And those who laugh with God have the capability of discovering that as well."

"I am beginning to understand this subject better, Flying Eagle, but I don't feel any closer to experiencing God's humor."

"Do you really want to experience his humor?"

"Well, the idea of exchanging a few jokes with Star Man seems O.K. to me now but I'm not so sure I am ready to be the brunt of one of God's practical jokes."

"But that is not a choice you have. You have already been the brunt of God's practical jokes many times; you just didn't know it. You did not know they were jokes and you did not laugh. Remember your flat tire in the rain on your trip out here? That joke was to make you look at yourself and to grow. The Spirit was preparing you for what you are learning now."

"Well, Flying Eagle, I do want to grow. I guess I am willing to be the brunt of a practical joke if it will help me do that. How do I learn how to laugh with God?"

"Follow the process of The Circumstances. If you follow that process you will discover that the Spirit is in everything that happens. That is the secret. There are no mere coincidences. Everything that happens is a result of the will of the Spirit and everything that happens can help you grow."

"That's it? There are no mere coincidences?"

"That is correct."

It struck me as funny. Nearly all of my life I had, in one way or another, been struggling with life and looking for God. The thought that God was already in everything that happened hit me as ironic, funny. I chuckled.

"You are on the way," he said. "You are beginning to experience the humor of it all. Stay with the process. It is just beginning." He stood up and walked away.

❧ 10 ❧

I chuckled; I snickered; I laughed out loud. The thought of my pursuing an intensive quest for the divine, while God was constantly, intensively, relating to me through all things, was hilarious. I saw my whole religious search as a cosmic practical joke on me. I had been allowed to search constantly for that which, or should I say, who, was constantly right under my nose. I was sure that God had been laughing. Now, at last, I was laughing with God about it.

I realized that something had shifted for me. I found that I was no longer taking life so seriously. And I was not taking myself so seriously either. I looked back over various times when a series of "circumstances" combined to produce some sort of disaster in my life. I had survived them all. I had not laughed, but I had survived. Could it be that they were not just a series of circumstances, that God had been active in them all, repeatedly giving me opportunities to look at myself or my conduct and to laugh with him? Many of the things I had gone through still did not seem funny to me. I had been through some very difficult times. In my religious upbringing I had been taught that one is supposed to learn to endure hardships. But Flying Eagle's teaching was radically different. Laughter, rather than mere endurance, was the goal.

But when I thought about Jesus' life and teachings, I did not see much humor. I asked Flying Eagle about that a few days later.

"You do not understand his teachings," Flying Eagle said. "You Christians keep trying to make Jesus into an example of how to live a holy life. You would do well to forget all that. Jesus' life is an example of how to live Jesus' life, not an example of how to live your life. You, my friend, are not Jesus. You are not called to be Jesus and you have misread the scriptures if you got that impression. Jesus was called to teach about the Kingdom of God and to die a sacrificial death. The scriptures proclaim that he was called to be the Messiah. If I am not mistaken you are not called to be the Messiah. And if you don't mind my saying so, I don't think you would make a particularly good Messiah. On the other hand, you would make an excellent Screaming Hawk.

So be Screaming Hawk. That is your calling now. Be yourself.

"And while I am on the subject of the Bible, there is something else that you Christians do with it that makes me very uneasy. I know that it bothers Star Man also. We have talked about it. You Christians keep trying to use the Bible as if it were a manual of rules and regulations that tells you how to live your lives. Much of Jesus' teaching was about throwing away the rules and living in a dynamic relationship with the Spirit. The Bible was never intended to be a rule book or to take the place of the Spirit in your life. You listen to the Bible instead of listening to the Spirit.

"One of the Spirit's functions is to teach you how to be yourself. The Bible is about people who listened to the Spirit and became themselves. But you Christians are always trying to be someone else. Most of you read the Bible to become like Jesus or Peter or Paul. Copying someone else or even listening to the Spirit's words to someone else is not the same as listening to the Spirit for oneself.

"During most of the history of Christianity most Christians did not own Bibles and most Christians did not even know how to read. Now that Bibles are relatively cheap and many people know how to read, many do read the Bible. That's fine. But you have made Christianity into a religion about reading the Bible. I have even heard some of your teachers say that you cannot be a good Christian unless you read the Bible an hour each day.

"Read the Bible. Study it. Learn about it. The Bible is inspired. But remember that through the centuries most Christians did not read the Bible and that Christianity is not really about relating to the Spirit through a book. Do not just read. You must learn to listen to the Spirit directly.

"You asked about humor in Jesus' life and teachings. Actually, there is more humor in the Bible and even in Jesus' sayings and parables than you might suppose, but you are correct that most of the Bible is not basically about humor. The Bible is not a guide book about how to experience God's humor. You will not discover it just by reading the Bible. But if you listen deeply enough to the Spirit, sooner or later you will discover God's humor. God's desire is to laugh with you. He laughs in the midst of adversity and he longs for you to learn how to laugh as well."

"Well, at least I have started to laugh with him about my search for him while he was constantly revealing himself to me."

"Yes, you are starting to experience the humor and, as you discovered, your own dynamics are what makes that situation funny. One must be able to laugh at himself in order to be able to laugh with God. If you had still been taking yourself and your quest so seriously you would not have been able to find the humor because you would not have been able to laugh at yourself. When you are so serious, you are living out of your thinking system. When people laugh, they are in touch with their feeling systems. Although you still have the habit of operating out of your thinking most of the time, you did manage to shift to your feeling system long enough to experience the humor this time.

"God prefers to communicate with people through their feeling systems. One of the ironies is that you Christians have tried so hard to develop a thinking man's religion. You think this or that is true about God. You teach your children what to think and you think thereby that you have taught them how to relate to God. But God is not impressed. God has never been particularly interested in working with people who rely on figuring things out about the Spirit instead of experiencing them. That is what Jesus meant when he said that you must enter the Kingdom of Heaven as a little child. Children encounter through their feeling system. Most adults try to encounter God through their thinking system. Frankly, God gets bored by that. Perhaps one reason that God is such a trickster is that you Christians bore him so much he needs some comic relief from time to time."

"I must say that I can understand that, Flying Eagle. I didn't find Christianity to be very stimulating the way it was presented to me when I was growing up."

"That's right. I bet your teachers tried to get you to think thoughts about God at a time when you were ready to experience God through your feelings. Educating children into a relationship with God never has worked. Allowing them to experience God through their feelings and then helping them to understand that which they have already experienced does work. Christians need to learn from their children how to encounter God. Thinking can be useful but experience needs to come first."

"How would you help children to experience God?"

"I am not a Christian. How I would do it is not the same as how you need to do it. My religion is about encountering the Spirit in nature. We encourage our children to experience the Spirit there first. Your religion is about encountering the Spirit in community. If I were a Christian, I would encourage the children to sense the presence of the Spirit in your gatherings. If you love each other, your children will sense that. If you do not love each other, your children will sense that also. To teach your children about the Spirit you must first build community among your people. Your gatherings for worship need to be places where all are accepted and loved as they are and where the children are valued for being themselves. Your children are the ones who can lead you most fully into an experience of the Spirit's presence because they experience without trying to figure things out first. To experience the Spirit in community one must be able to put all ideas of God aside and to experience what is there rather than what one thinks should be there. Children respond to what is, rather than to what people think about what is. The children can sense the Spirit's presence in your gatherings. The children can tell you when you truly love one another. Love, though not a feeling, can be encountered through the feeling system and your children will experience it in your gatherings if it is real. Let them experience the presence of the Spirit first. Then help them to understand what they have experienced. Just to teach them what you think about the Spirit is not effective.

"But I must warn you about something that is very important. You are starting once again to get into your intellect and to think too much about this subject. You must learn to listen to the Spirit. You are still trying to figure everything out. Although you are just starting to experience God's humor it is essential that you also start experiencing the Fifth Path, The Path of Illumination. Unless you start experiencing illumination you will lose the progress that you have made. Tomorrow I will teach you about illumination."

❧ 11 ❧

I was awakened by a knock on my door.

"Yes?" I called out into the darkness.

"It is time to get up. We have much work to do today." It was Flying Eagle. I glanced at the alarm clock on the table beside my bed. Two A.M. I dressed quickly and met him outside.

"What's going on?" I asked sleepily.

"I am here to teach you about the Path of Illumination. No more questions.

"Leave your flashlight here. You will not be needing it and there is no point in carrying things on a journey that you do not need. But you will need one sock and a handkerchief. That is very important."

I returned the flashlight to my room, stuffed one sock and a handkerchief into my pocket and rejoined Flying Eagle.

"Follow me," he said. "And don't ask me any questions while we are in the forest. I must concentrate."

We moved off by the light of the moon and stars. The moonlight made it easy to find our way through the village and to the head of the trail; but, once we entered the forest the heavy foliage blocked out most of the light, and we were plunged into nearly total darkness. We walked for a couple of hours. Flying Eagle confidently led the way at a brisk pace with me stumbling along behind. I was amazed that he was able to follow the winding trail through the forest. I had to strain even to see his light-colored jacket and at times I had to follow him more from the sound of his footsteps than from any visual cues. I frequently tripped on roots and stones. Flying Eagle never faltered and his pace never slackened.

"How can you see in this darkness?" I blurted out after one of my falls.

"No questions!" he replied curtly.

I stumbled on in silence. Finally we emerged into the moonlight again. We were on the edge of a clearing at the top of a large hill.

"We will stop here for a while. I will answer your questions now," he said.

"How could you see that trail in the dark?"

"I couldn't."

"How did you follow it then?"

"I remembered it."

"You remembered it?"

"Yes. I have been down this trail before. I was here just last month."

"We must have come five or six miles. How can you remember all those twists and turns?"

"My mind does not remember. My body does. And your body does too. I will show you."

He led me back into the forest on the trail that we had just taken. Then he stopped, took the handkerchief that I had brought along, made a blindfold and tied it over my eyes.

"Can you see anything?" he asked.

"Of course not. I could hardly see anything before the blindfold. It's too dark."

"The blindfold makes it easier the first time. This way you will not be tempted to try to see. I want you to feel the trail not see it."

He walked around behind me.

"You are pointed in the right direction. Now you lead the way back."

I paused and then took a few faltering steps.

"Stop," he said. "The trail turns here. Can you feel it?"

I couldn't feel anything.

"Get quiet and center yourself. We will wait here. Tell me when you can feel the trail."

I got quiet within. I gradually became less aware of the blindfold over my eyes. I started to be aware of a slight sensation in my legs, a feeling that is hard to describe other than to say that they wanted to turn slightly to the right.

"Can you feel the trail yet?"

"I think I am starting to. I think it turns a little to the right here."

"That's right. Lead on."

I moved out gingerly. I took perhaps ten steps and then stopped abruptly. Flying Eagle ran into the back of me.

"Why did you stop?"

"My mind is saying that this is crazy. I don't remember the trail."

"Don't pay attention to your mind. Your mind does not remember the trail. Your body does. Lead on."

I took a minute to center myself again and then moved forward. My legs were leading me. I could feel where they wanted to go. I made a turn to the left and then, after about twenty steps, another gradual turn to the right. I was really feeling the trail. I was starting to feel a sense of confidence when suddenly I stopped again. I felt anxious.

"What happened?" I said. "I can't feel the trail any more."

"This is one of the places where you fell."

I inched forward, feeling around carefully with my feet. I made contact with a large rock jutting up out of the ground. I stepped over the rock and cautiously started moving forward again. The sensation in my legs returned and I could feel the trail once more.

"Let me make a suggestion," he said. "It is easier if you walk fast. Your body is constantly having to make adjustments because you are walking more slowly now than you were when you followed me along the trail."

I took his advice and picked up the pace. I found he was right. It was easier. The sensations in my legs were stronger and I actually felt more secure walking fast than I had when walking slowly. I was amazed by how easy it was. We walked for perhaps an hour. Other than stopping at each of the places where I had previously stumbled, I followed the winding trail without difficulty and was actually enjoying myself. When Flying Eagle told me to stop walking I felt disappointed.

"It is time to get rid of the blindfold," he said as he untied the handkerchief from around my eyes.

When I opened my eyes I could see the trail in the dim light of the dawning day.

"I want you to walk using your eyes now," he said.

"Why?"

"Because I do not want to be late for breakfast."

"What?"

"I do not want to be late for breakfast. There are things that I need to tell you. If you are wearing the blindfold you must concentrate on the feelings that you have in your legs and we will not be able to talk as we walk. If we stop to talk we will not be back in time.

"I really like you." He paused a moment. "Well, perhaps I should say in all honesty that sometimes I really like you. But you are not someone for whom I would be willing to miss my breakfast."

"Thanks a lot!"

He chuckled and gave me an affectionate squeeze with one arm around my shoulders. We started walking toward the village again.

"How was it for you to walk without using your eyes?"

"I loved it. I didn't want to stop."

"It is nice, isn't it? But you have to be careful about two things."

"Oh? What's that?"

"Fallen limbs and moose droppings. Never wear your best shoes if you are going to walk down a trail blindfolded," he said pointing to my soiled shoes. "Moose are wonderful animals, but they are not always considerate of the humans who share these trails with them. I had a conversation with a moose about the problem once."

"What did he say?"

"He said that he had no intention of mending his ways and that if I did not like the condition in which he left the trails that I could walk with my eyes open. He had a point.

"But there are other things besides moose that we need to talk about. I told you that you must follow the Path of Illumination. Following that Path is very much like following a trail without using your eyes. You must rely on your feelings.

"Some think that the Path of Illumination is a path to new knowledge. It is not. It is a path to the memories that are within you that you can not remember with your mind. There is much knowledge that you have within you. It is not new knowledge. It is very old knowledge. Through the Path of Illumination one starts to remember consciously the truths which are stored in the deeper recesses of their being. The key to that process is one's feelings. One must start trusting what one's feelings are saying about the nature of reality and other universal truths. One who follows that path discovers truths that are deeper than words and that are beyond one's normal memories."

"I don't understand. You say that these truths are memories. If someone told me these things why can't I remember them?"

"You were not told these things. They are part of your being. Just as your body remembered the trail that you have been following blindfolded, your being can remember truths that you experienced before your physical conception into this life. The memories are there. They can be brought into consciousness but only by trusting the feelings that are deep within you. They are memories. They have to do with how you experienced reality prior to entering this life. Some are your own personal memories but others are memories that are shared by all human beings. Your personal memories regard the nature of your own specific encounters with the Spirit but the broader memories are of the path followed by all mankind moving through the ages toward reunion with the Spirit. Your being remembers much about the Spirit. Much of what I have been teaching you your being already knew. The teachings seemed new but also familiar, did they not?"

"Yes, they did."

"In this life you had not heard them before; but, on a deeper level, you already knew them. Your being remembered. That feeling of recognition deep within you is your being remembering what you already know."

"If I already know these things why do I have to be taught them by you or anyone else? Why can't I just go within and discover them again for myself?"

At that he stopped dead in his tracks. He turned toward me grinning broadly.

"You got it, Screaming Hawk! That is exactly what I have been trying to get across to you this morning. I was trying to show you that the memories are within you and that you can rediscover them for yourself without my assistance. When you are following the Path of Illumination the memories of previously known truths come back to you without the assistance of another person's teachings. Many of the Christian mystics of the past went into solitude to learn the truths that were within them.

"But on a more practical note, it is not always convenient to rely solely on the Path of Illumination to regain one's knowledge of the truth. That path takes much concentration. To regain all one's knowledge in that fashion requires retreating from the world for long periods of time and devoting oneself almost exclusively to the task. It is just like walking through the forest blindfolded. You can do that, as you have experienced this morning, but you must concentrate solely on that task. If you try to do other things at the same time, like talking, you will lose the trail and walk into a tree. Because the Path of Illumination requires total concentration, I suggest that you follow that Path at times, but that you not follow it exclusively. Listen to the teachings of others also. That too can hasten the return of many of the memories that you share with others. There is, however, a limit to what you can learn through listening to others. Some knowledge is stored among your personal memories. That knowledge is yours alone and cannot be remembered by listening to others. To access your personal knowledge, follow The Path of Illumination.

"Some of what I just told you may be confusing. Your confusion is not important. If you remember to listen to others *and* to follow The Path of Illumination, the proper memories will return to you when they are needed. Is that clear?"

"Yes."

We were nearing the village. I could detect a faint scent of smoke carried on the gentle morning breeze.

"I have two more questions," I said. "First, why is it so important to follow the Path of Illumination when I am experiencing the Path of Humor?"

"Because the Path of Illumination will provide you with a balance. Many lose sight of some of the deeper truths when they discover divine humor. They start trying to relate to the Spirit exclusively through humor and their growth is hampered. No one Path is the exclusive path to wholeness. They must be used in combination. Those who rely too heavily on only one path lack balance. Some things can be experienced on the Path of Humor, other things on the Path of Illumination; but, unless you keep a balance, you run the risk of becoming so heavenly minded that you are no earthly good. Balance is essential. It is balance that allows a person to be both in the world and not of the world.

"It is time for breakfast. What is your second question?"

"Why did you tell me to bring along one sock?"

"In order to provide a little balance to this otherwise rather serious morning. Look inside it."

I pulled the sock out of my pocket, and stuck my hand into it, and pulled out a small note.

"Sorry about your shoes," it said, "but remember, only a fool walks through the forest with his eyes closed." It was signed, "The Moose."

I chuckled and headed for the dining hall with Flying Eagle.

"I just had an awful thought," he said. "What if Buffalo Woman is cooking this morning."

God was merciful. Not only did Buffalo Woman not cook that morning but we were informed that she had gone to visit her niece and would be away for several weeks. Everyone breathed a sigh of relief. Someone suggested that special prayers be offered for the niece. But Flying Eagle himself said that the suggestion to send a letter to the niece expressing the gratitude of the village was inappropriate.

❧ 12 ❧

I took a long nap after breakfast and met with Flying Eagle again in the afternoon.

"You did well this morning," he said. "I once had a student who left the trail over a dozen times on his first walk with a blindfold. Not only did we miss breakfast but at times I wondered if we would make it back for lunch. Star Man was right. You are more ready to learn these things than I thought.

"It is important now to practice the Paths that you have learned thus far and to make them a part of the rhythm of your life. It is then that you will start to discover the full power of the Circumstances. The Spirit acts most powerfully not in the peculiar happenings that many refer to as 'miracles' but in the regular coincidences and circumstances in life. As you practice the paths you will find that your life works, that solutions to difficult problems will often come about with little or no effort on your part as a result of circumstances. You will see that happen over and over again and you will come to expect it. That is part of what is meant by living by faith. One reaches the point where one expects the Spirit to work through all things. Your religion teaches that 'in everything God works for good with those who love him, who are called according to his purposes.' That really is true. The Spirit has called you and you will discover the full power of that statement as you trust it and follow The Paths.

"I have not taught you all there is to know about the Paths. You will have more questions as you continue to practice the Paths. I will answer them later as they arise.

"Practicing all the other Paths will lead you to the final Path that you must learn, the Path of Indifference. This path is not generally held in high regard by those in your religion, but it is very important. It is the path that Christians needed to learn from the Stoics. But instead of learning from them, the Christians declared Stoic teachings to be anathema and proclaimed that nothing of value could be learned from them. During much of the history of Christianity, most Christians have rejected the teachings found in other religons. But, as I told you last summer, Christianity is not complete in itself.

It must absorb the important truths of other religions before it will be complete. The Stoics had much to teach the Christians about the truth and, likewise, there was much that the Stoics could have learned from the Christian revelation.

"The Stoic teachings were misunderstood by Christians and even by many Stoics. Some thought that the teachings about indifference encouraged the denial of one's feelings and led to a lack of concern about action. I must warn you that there are many today who will misunderstand your teachings if you are not extremely careful about what you say regarding the Path of Indifference.

"Just as the Path of Humor is dangerous if it is incorrectly applied, the Path of Indifference is dangerous if one tries to follow it too early in the course of one's spiritual development. This is the last path. You must practice the others first. If you follow the Path of Indifference too early, it can lead to inactivity or denial of feelings; but, practiced last, it can bring about a harmony of the other paths and you will find yourself at one with the mind of the Creator. True indifference is not the absence of caring. True indifference is living out of the knowledge that the will of the Creator is in all things and in all circumstances, and that if one lives according to the Spirit one need not be concerned about the outcome of any event.

"If true indifference is not achieved by simply not caring, how do you follow the Path?"

"When one achieves true indifference, he becomes one with the Spirit. I can not tell you how to do that. You must experience it. All I can tell you is that it is possible after you have followed the other paths. Seek indifference at that point and you will discover it.

"We have talked enough for today. Too much information in one day is not good. I will tell you more tomorrow."

❧ 13 ❧

The next day he returned to the subject.

"I have taught you about all of the Paths. I have talked about some Paths in more detail than others because they were new to your conscious mind. Others, such as The Path of Silence, were already somewhat familiar to you. You must practice the paths now. It is in the doing that true learning occurs. The paths will seem both new and familiar as you start remembering that which is in your being. None of what I have taught you about the Circumstances is new knowledge. It has been present and available to all through the ages. That it has been ignored is largely a result of fear. People fear the Spirit. Union with the Spirit is feared as though it were death. People fear that they will lose their own identity if they become one with the Spirit. Telling them that they will find their true identity in the Spirit does not remove that fear. If you teach others about The Paths you will encounter great resistance. You, too, have been resisting these teachings have you not?"

"No. I have been very interested in what you have been teaching me."

"I have not been teaching you these things in order to interest you. You think that your interest indicates that you are open to these teachings. It does not."

"But I feel open. Why do you say that I am resistant?"

"Your feelings are not always an indicator of true openness either. I have been teaching you about the Paths for several days. During that time, how much have you been practicing them?"

I opened my mouth and was about to defend myself by saying that I always put his teachings into practice. But I stopped short. I realized to my surprise that he was right. I had not practiced them. I had thought about what he was teaching me. I had been interested in what he told me and was also anxious to hear what he would say next, but I had not put any of the teachings into action. I had not even continued my regular practice of Silence during the last few days.

"You are right! I haven't practiced the Paths. I just realized that I haven't even continued my practice of Silence. I must be resisting something."

"In your culture people frequently confuse interest with commitment," he continued. "Many people are interested in religion. They think about it, read about it, even study it in depth, but they continue to be resistant to making its teachings a part of their life. Interest is not openness. Interest is interest, nothing more.

"You have been interested in The Paths but you have not practiced them because you are afraid. You do not trust the Spirit. You hide your fear behind interest and continue to operate in the realm of your mind. These teachings are not for your mind. What you think about these teachings has no value. The courage to remember and to experience again the ways of the Spirit is all that is important.

"Until you reach the point that you are ready to put The Paths into practice, further talk will be a waste of time. Come find me when you are ready to act. In the meantime, take your interest and go." He turned abruptly and walked away.

I struggled internally for the next two days. I knew it was time to put his teachings into action. But I was starting to feel the fear he had identified within me. Was I afraid that union with the Spirit would lead to a loss of my own identity? The more I pondered the question the more my anxiety increased. I wanted the Spirit to remove, or at least reduce, my inadequacies but I did not want to lose my identity in the process. Flying Eagle said that one finds one's true self in the Spirit. What if he is wrong? What if that union obliterates all awareness of oneself forever? Did I want that? Definitely not!

The fear persisted. It even intensified. Is the Spirit really loving? Can I trust the Spirit with my being? I had been told all my life, in one way or another, that the Spirit could be trusted, but I found that it was one thing to intellectually accept the concept that God is good and quite another to feel with certainty that God is good. It is like the situation faced by people who intellectually believe there is an after life and yet still feel fear when facing their own imminent death. Knowing something intellectually and knowing it with one's being are two different things. It seemed that the only way to find out whether I could trust the Spirit with my being was to trust that which I did not trust. Although I was still afraid, I did trust Flying Eagle. He believed the Spirit to be trustworthy and I found that I was able to trust his trust of the Spirit, even though I was not yet able to trust the Spirit directly myself. Deep trust of Flying Eagle became the basis of a rather tentative, but nonetheless real, trust of the Spirit. I was now ready to act.

I went to look for Flying Eagle. I found him sitting in a chair on the porch to his lodge. He was reading another mystery novel. He looked up as I walked over to him.

"I knew it!" he exclaimed. "I was just about to find out whether or not the butler really did it. It never fails! I always get interrupted at the best part!"

"Do you want me to come back later?"

"No. It wouldn't do any good. If it weren't you the Spirit would send somebody else to interrupt me."

"Did it ever occur to you that the Spirit might not like his medicine men reading mystery novels during working hours?"

"Of course it has occurred to me. Why do you think I do it?"

"I must say that you have a strange relationship with the Spirit, Flying Eagle."

"The Spirit and I understand each other. I let the Spirit be the Spirit and the Spirit lets me be me, at least most of the time. I like to eat and I like to read mystery novels and sometimes I get bored at the ceremonies. I know all that does not quite fit the image of a medicine man but that's who I am. I talked to the Spirit about it and the Spirit said that it is much more important for me to be myself than it is for me to live up to other people's expectations of me. Part of who I am is a feisty old man who likes to do things his own way. The Spirit understands that and plays along by interrupting me when I am reading. It's no fun to be feisty unless there is someone to be feisty with. So the Spirit and I stay in conflict about mystery novels and about my doing crossword puzzles at the ceremonies. We enjoy it and it keeps us from being in conflict about things that are more important."

"I see.

"Flying Eagle, there is something I have wondered about. How do you work crossword puzzles in you head?"

"It takes a lot of preparation. First, I memorize all the clues for down and across. That is the hardest part. Memorizing the layout of the blocks is easier because I can visualize that part. It takes a while but it's worth it. The Spirit really gets upset with me about it.

"Once I made up a cross word puzzle during an extra long ceremony. It was pretty good. I even sent it off to one of those magazines. They wrote back and thanked me for the submission but said that there were too many ceremonial words in it. I wrote back and said that I had designed the puzzle to be used during solemn ceremonies. They didn't print the puzzle and they never wrote back. They must have thought that I was some kind of a kook."

He sighed and shook his head sadly. Then he looked up at me again.

"Have you come to me because you are ready to practice The Paths now?"

"Yes."

"Good," he said. "Then go sit in the forest and get started."

"I do have a question though. May I ask it now?"

"You might as well. You have already interrupted me," he said, with a little twinkle in his eye.

"I noticed that being taught that the Spirit is loving was not enough for me to really trust the Spirit. It was my trust in your trust of the Spirit that has allowed me to start trusting the Spirit. Am I peculiar?"

"Yes, you are peculiar," he said with a smile, "but no, you are not peculiar in that particular area.

"A person can think things by himself. But true faith is never experienced in isolation. Faith in the goodness of the Spirit is never solely one's own. It is a joint memory on the being level that is shared with all other people and it is encountered when people remember together. We share a common faith; we do not experience it as individuals nor can we contact that memory in isolation from others. Do you understand?"

"Not really."

"It always surprises me that Christians seem to have so much difficulty with this concept. Much of your religion is about this. Your religion talks about the Church, a body of people who share a common faith, a memory from their being level. Your worship services are about gathering together in order to remember together. That is at the very heart of your communion service. 'Do this in remembrance of me' is not an empty statement. It is the very heart of your worship. Remembrance is that special kind of remembering that reaches down into the level of being and contacts the pool of common memories. The group remembers together. When that is done, faith is shared and the power associated with those memories is available in the present. Contrary to what you may have been taught as a child, Christianity is not primarily about experiencing one's personal relationship with God. While it is true that a person can experience God as an individual, Christianity is primarily about the encounter with God in community.

"In my culture we talk about the importance of being in a tribe. Our common memories are important. Just as one can not truly be an Indian without being a member of a tribe, one can not truly be a Christian in isolation from others either.

"You have discovered the importance of community. You found you could not even believe in the goodness of the Spirit in isolation. It was my faith that helped you remember your faith. It is always that way. Faith is encountered in community even if that community is only two or three people or, in this case, a student and his teacher. One cannot go it alone. One must have others in order to encounter the group memory. One's memory of one's faith comes in response to the memory of others and their faith in turn comes from sharing in the memory of others. That is the way it is. Faith is always in response to the faith of others.

"Part of your problem is that those of your faith have replaced the understanding of the God of the people with the idea of a personal God of the individual. In doing that, you have lost your understanding of the power of the revelation of God to a people and you have lost the experience of God in the midst of community. Reinterpreting Christianity as a religion that is primarily about one's private relationship with God is a great disservice in the long run. It has robbed your religion of much of its power. The experience of God comes to the individual but the revelation of God comes to a people."

"I'm not sure that I understand the difference."

"You will, but not today. We have talked enough today. You need to practice The Paths and I need to find out whether or not the butler did it. We will talk more later."

He picked up his book and started reading again. As I was approaching the edge of the forest I heard Flying Eagle's voice and looked back.

"I knew it! I knew it!" he exclaimed. He was still reading his novel. He was grinning, chuckling and rocking back and forth in his chair in sheer delight. I left the world of mystery novels and eccentric medicine men behind and entered the world of the animals. The next phase of my own mysterious journey toward union with the Spirit was underway.

❦ 14 ❦

The forest that so many times before had been a place of quiet solitude and peace now seemed hostile. I felt out of place as I walked along the trail. The sounds of the animals seemed like reminders that I was a stranger treading on their territory with expectations and values that were foreign to them.

I sat down on the trunk of a fallen tree near the trail and tried to focus on Flying Eagle's teachings. I thought about The Paths. Most of all I tried to think about the Path of the Greatest Good. I seemed to be getting nowhere. The longer I sat the more uncomfortable and out of place I felt.

Two hours or more went by. I was in agony. I debated about returning to the village, but I had come to practice The Paths. To return at this point would have been an admission of defeat. I stayed on.

Eventually, it occurred to me to call on my power animal. I closed my eyes, focused on the hawk and waited in the agonizing silence. Nothing.

Finally, as I was about to give up, I heard the gentle fluttering sound of wings beating the air. I opened my eyes and saw the hawk landing a few feet in front of me.

He looked at me for a minute or two and then spoke.

"You always seem to do things the hard way," he said. There was no sound but his voice was unmistakable and as clear as if he had used his vocal cords. "You try to do alone that which can not be done without The Presence."

"The Presence? What Presence?" I asked.

"The Presence of the Spirit. You act as if The Paths that you are trying to follow are your paths. They are not. They are the Spirit's paths. You have been invited to join the Spirit on the journey. The Spirit will not follow along behind you on your path, but the Spirit will allow you to become a companion on the Spirit's path.

"You have been sitting here alone in the forest trying to follow The Path as though it were yours alone. You have been trying to make a journey alone that can only be made with a companion. The Path of the Greatest Good is not the path of your greatest good. Don't you understand that yet? It is the path of the Spirit's greatest good. The Inner Journey, Silence, Humor,

Illumination and Indifference, all of them are the Spirit's Paths, not yours. If you are ever on any of those paths, you are there by invitation, because the Spirit has invited you to come along. You have been treating this as though it were your private journey. You must practice solitude not aloneness."

"But I thought solitude was aloneness. What's the difference?"

"What's the difference?" There was a tone in his voice of utter disbelief that I was asking the question. "What's the difference?" he said again. "They are opposites. Surely you know that!"

"In what way are they opposites?" I asked, feeling like a complete fool.

The hawk walked around in a tight circle then paused and looked at me again.

"You are serious. I can tell that you are serious," he said and then paused. "You really are serious, aren't you?"

"Yes, I'm serious," I said angrily. "I'm dumb, stupid, ignorant and I don't know anything, alright? I don't know the difference and I'm asking you to tell me."

"Alright, forgive me. Sometimes I forget that being human means living in a state of limited knowledge and that humans sometimes have to learn the most basic of principles through experience rather than direct knowledge. Being a power animal isn't easy, you know. Its not easy teaching someone how to be human when one has never been human oneself. One tends to assume that universal knowledge is known by all creatures. I forget that humans cannot always remember what their being knows.

"Aloneness is being by oneself. Solitude is entering into a partnership with the Spirit. Spiritual growth does not come out of aloneness. None of the spiritual principles are expected to be practiced out of aloneness. No growth ever occurs except in partnership. It is one of the most basic principles of the universe. You fear union with the Spirit but there is no other way to grow. Union with the Spirit is life. Aloneness is death. You seem to think that if you maintain your aloneness you are free to be yourself. You can only be yourself in partnership. Solitude is partnership with the Spirit. Fellowship is being in partnership with other people. If you want life, you must choose partnership. You can only know yourself in relationship. All animals know that. We live in relationship to the Spirit. There is no other way."

"Is that what is meant by having a personal relationship with God?"

"Yes, but I must caution you that many people think of it as their relationship with God, as though they own it. One does not own the Spirit and one can not ever, through any action, earn a relationship with the Spirit. The Spirit gives. The relationship is by invitation. You can not earn the relationship by anything that you do, including practicing The Paths. Do you understand?"

"Well if I can't earn it, why am I out here trying to practice the Path of the Greatest Good?"

"That was exactly the question that I was going to ask you. Why are you here?"

I thought for a few minutes.

"Well, I guess I am here to do what I need to do in order to deepen my relationship with the Spirit."

"But you can not do that."

"What do you mean?"

"Just what I said, you can not do that. You can not, through anything that you do, deepen a relationship that can not be earned. The relationship is not earned. It is offered but it can not be earned. You do not yet understand the full implications of that, do you?

"Look, do you think I became a bird by working at it?

"I became a bird by being a bird. You become a human by being a human. You did not earn it. You can not earn it and you can not make it happen. To be human is to live in relationship. You have an invitation to relate to the Spirit because being human means living in relationship. There is no other way to be human. Not to live in relationship is to deny your humanity. You can not do anything to earn a relationship with the Spirit; you can only be in relationship with the Spirit. As long as you are trying to be in that which you already are, you are not being in that which you are."

"I'm not sure I followed that last sentence."

"To be human is to be in relationship with the Spirit. It is part of being human. It is your natural state of being. When you are not in relationship with the Spirit you are not human. It is union with the Spirit that makes you human. When you try to be that which you already are, you cannot be that which you are. You are in union with the Spirit. You are moving in the direction of awareness of that which already is. The Spirit invited you into union when you were created. Your task is to discover the union that is already there. When you deny that union, you deny your humanity. When you try to earn that union with the Spirit through your actions, you are denying that which already is. Trying to follow the Paths in order to relate to the Spirit denies the relationship that already exists. Trying to relate to the Spirit prevents you from relating to the Spirit. You are the Spirit. The Spirit is in you and you are in the Spirit. Religion is not about the quest for God. It is about the discovery of what already is. In your religion you do not become the body of Christ, you recognize that you always have been the body of Christ. Trying to become the body of Christ prevents you from living out of what you already are. When you are trying to become that which you already are, you are not able to be yourself.

"I have put it to you in a number of different ways. Are you starting to get it now or do I need to continue?"

"I think I am starting to get it. I have been afraid of union with the Spirit because I thought it was something different from the state that I already was in. Because I was continuing to think of union with the Spirit as something that had not already occurred, I was not able to experience the union that already exists. Union was given to me at creation. I am already in union with the Spirit."

"You understand. Now I have a question for you. Since the union with the Spirit already exists, how do you go about practicing The Paths?"

"By recognizing that The Paths are the Spirit's, and that I am already in union with the Spirit, and that practicing the Paths is an expression of the union that already exists rather than a pathway to that union."

"That is correct. Now go to it."

The bird leaped into the air and flew off through the trees.

❧ 15 ❧

I sat and thought about the implications of what the hawk had told me. I had thought that consistently following The Paths would eventually result in my union with the Spirit. But I now realized that following the Paths does not create the union; it helps one recognize and express the union that already exists.

My thoughts turned to the matter of the Greatest Good. Since the Spirit and I are in union, the Spirit's greatest good and my greatest good are the same. As I discover the Spirit more fully, I am also discovering myself more fully. When I deal with myself as though my will and needs are different from the Spirit's, I am acting out of an illusion rather than reality. Flying Eagle said that rather than losing myself in the union with the Spirit that I would find myself. I was beginning to understand what he meant.

The Greatest Good is not my good as a separate being but my good as experienced in union with the Spirit. It is our greatest good. I had not thought of myself in the plural before but "we" was starting to make more sense than "I." Jesus certainly thought of himself as "we" rather than "I." Could it have been his humanity speaking when Jesus said, "I and the Father are one"? Is that union with the Father true for all of us? To act out of the Greatest Good is to follow the will of the Spirit, but the Spirit's will and my will, devoid of the illusion that I am an individual, are the same.

So what is the Path of the Greatest Good for my life? What do I, in the depths of my plural being, want to do with my life? The answer tumbled out even as I asked the question. I want to dedicate my life to teaching. But I do not want to teach traditional theology. I want my students to experience the kinds of things that I have been learning from Flying Eagle and I want to assist them with the process of discovering and experiencing the truth both in and outside of traditional Christianity.

I thought about my current teaching position at the college and the kind of conflicts that I was already having with the department head. I realized that it would be impossible for me to pursue a truly creative, experiential approach to the teaching of religion while in his department. If I were to pursue the greatest good I would need to find a new setting in which to teach. I started to think about how I might go about looking for a new position. Then my heart sank. I had already signed a contract for the coming school year. If I were to keep that commitment, it would mean staying in my present position for another year. If I broke that contract at this point, it would not reflect well on me with either my present employer or a future one. I seemed to be stuck in my present situation for the time being. I truly did want to pursue the Greatest Good but circumstances were keeping me stuck in my present job. I felt frustrated.

At that point it started to rain. I decided to return to the forest the next day and headed back to the village.

When I reached my room there was a letter waiting for me from the president of the college. It started out with the usual sort of opening niceties about hoping that I was enjoying the summer, etc. and then got down to the heart of the matter.

> John Wilson called me last week and indicated that due to circumstances beyond his control he must resign his position as head of the Religion Department and return to Iowa in order to take care of his elderly mother. In the light of this turn of events, I would like to explore your thoughts about the current and future needs of the department. I particularly would like to hear any thoughts you may have regarding a suggestion that we restructure the Religion Department along less traditional lines and offer some courses that are more experiential in nature.
>
> Please call me collect at your earliest convenience.

My head was spinning. The phrase from the letter, "due to circumstances beyond his control," kept running through my head. I had to talk to Flying Eagle!

I found him on the porch of his lodge.

"I knew it!" he screamed, throwing the mystery novel at me in mock rage. "This better be good!"

"I need to talk to you," I said, ignoring his theatrics.

I told him about my realization that the Greatest Good for me, at this point in my life, is to be a teacher of experience-oriented religion. And I explained that I could see no way to do that while working with the present department head. Then I showed him the letter. He read it and smiled.

"This is the work of the Spirit," he said. "You are starting to discover the power of Divine Circumstance.

"I have one suggestion, Screaming Hawk."

"What's that?"

"That you accept the position of Chairman of the Religion Department."

"But they are not offering it to me."

He smiled slyly. "They will. The Spirit told me last week."

❧ 16 ❧

I hung up the phone after an hour and a half of conversation with the president of the college. Flying Eagle had been right as usual. After a long discussion about the needs of the department and questions about the kind of courses I thought should be offered, the president asked me if I would be interested in being the head of the department. The president said he liked my ideas and wanted to see them implemented. I accepted the position. It meant that I would need to return to the college a month earlier than I had originally planned and that I would have to make some short trips to interview some possible candidates for the current opening we had in the department. The president and I could come up with only three people worth considering who might be available to make a move on such short notice.

Later that evening I saw Flying Eagle.

"Did you accept the position?" he asked.

"Yes."

"Good. The Spirit really wants you to be the department head. If you had turned it down there would have been a series of circumstances that would have given you the opportunity to reconsider. Of course you still could have turned it down. You are never forced to follow the Path of the Greatest Good. It is always a free choice. But it is amazing how circumstances will open up opportunities when one is truly committed to that Path. Sometimes the Spirit acts by doing miraculous things, things that are impossible in your present system, but most of the time the Spirit acts through ordinary circumstances such as those you just encountered."

"If the Spirit is capable of making anything happen directly, why does the Spirit choose to use circumstances?"

"I do not know. Most of the time I cannot figure the Spirit out. It has taken me a long time to admit that to myself and others. A medicine man builds his reputation by knowing things about the Spirit that others do not know. I used to think from time to time that I had figured the Spirit out and could explain why the Spirit did things a certain way. I even thought I could predict what the Spirit would do next. But nearly every time I made a prediction the Spirit would do something that would totally surprise me. The Spirit remains a mystery to me. My suggestion is that you handle rather gently any explanation that you come up with to explain the Spirit's actions. Treat it like the fragile shell of a bird's egg. If you start treating any explanation like it is solid and dependable it may crumble in front of you.

"Theologians often try to explain why the Spirit does what the Spirit does. But theology is never more than a pointer in the direction of the truth. Great harm is done when one takes a theological statement as though it were the truth.

"Do not be certain about anything regarding the Spirit. Do not even be certain of the Spirit's existence. True faith is not knowing the truth and casting out doubt. Faith is choosing to act in accord with the deeper levels of one's being. It is on that level that you have encountered the Spirit and it is on that level that you have known the Spirit. Even so, doubts remain. Do not do away with them. Merely align yourself with the experience of your being and live out of that level of awareness. Allow the doubts in your mind to remain."

"Aren't you certain of the Spirit's existence?"

"No. I have had many experiences with the Spirit but I cannot prove the Spirit's existence even to myself. It is like your experience of The Greatest Good. You believe that The Greatest Good for you is to be a teacher dedicated to helping students experience the Spirit. You did not come to that conclusion through logic. Your intellect did not tell you that is The Greatest Good for you. You learned it through tapping the deeper levels of your being. It is your being that recognizes The Greatest Good and it is your being that recognizes the Spirit. You have chosen to align with what your being is telling you. It is the same way with knowledge of the Spirit. One cannot know that the Spirit exists through one's intellect. The proper stance to have is to choose to follow your heart with certainty while allowing your mind to have doubts. True faith always involves that choice."

"I was always taught that faith meant doing away with doubts. I'm still having a little trouble accepting that it is the way you describe it."

"Look, Screaming Hawk, if I suddenly came at you with a knife and told you that I was going to kill you, what would you do?"

"Well, I'm not sure. I don't believe that you would really try to kill me." ·

"Why?"

"Because I know you pretty well and I don't think that you really want to hurt me."

"But you are relying on your experience of me. Do you know with absolute certainty that I am not a secret murderer who sometimes brings his students to an untimely end if they question what I am telling them? At the point that I was coming at you with a knife would you be certain, without any doubts at all, that I would not kill you? When I raised the knife and started plunging it toward your heart would you not have an impulse to grab my arm and protect yourself?"

"Yes, I probably would have that impulse."

"You would have to make a choice between trusting your experience of me and those doubts in your mind that would make you tempted to defend yourself from my knife.

"I will go get my knife if you would like to find out what you would do."

"No, that's not necessary."

"Good. Through the years I have killed three students that way, but I really don't feel like killing another one today." He smiled.

My deeper self believed that he was joking about killing his students. But I wasn't sure I would be so confident if his knife really were coming toward me.

"There is something that still puzzles me," I said. "If the Spirit is really as you say, a mystery, why is it that there is so much in the Bible and other religious literature about the Spirit?"

"I don't understand your question, Screaming Hawk."

"If the Spirit is by nature a mystery why is revelation of the Spirit such a strong theme in religious literature?"

"The mystery lies within us, not within the Spirit. The Spirit does not mind your understanding why things are the way they are, but we are not able to understand many of the things that the Spirit is more than ready to reveal to us. The problem is that words can not adequately express most of the truths of the Spirit realm. Religious writings are usually attempts to put into words things which can not be adequately expressed in words. That is why placing too much emphasis on the words contained in religious writings can be a problem. Words do not tell the truth. At best they only point toward the truth. The truth is experienced. It is not grasped with the mind. People through the years have repeatedly tried to turn their religions into something that can be grasped with the mind. All religions are untrue on that level. Experience cannot be adequately put into words for the mind. Treating words of experience as though they were words for the mind is one of the greatest abuses of religion. And it is an abuse found in nearly all religions. The Spirit must be experienced. The Spirit can not be understood. Seeking understanding is not the path to the Spirit. And thinking that religious writings must be understood is folly."

"But isn't there value in studying religions?"

"Yes, of course, but not because it will lead you into an encounter with the

Spirit. No one has ever learned their way into an encounter with the Spirit. The purpose of religious writings is to help people vaguely understand what they have already experienced. The core of every religion is experience, not understanding of the Spirit, and you will never truly understand beyond the level of your experience. To know is to experience. Knowing does not come through understanding.

"Everyone already has a wealth of religious experience. Living is itself an encounter with the Spirit. The problem is that most people do not recognize their encounters with the Spirit. The Spirit is in everything and is in every experience of life. Your role as a teacher is to help your students come to the point that they can understand what they are experiencing, or to put it another way, to experience what they are already experiencing."

"To experience what they are already experiencing?"

"Yes. To help their being level align with their conscious level so they are operating as a unit. True spirituality is the experience of wholeness, of one's conscious awareness and one's deeper level of being coming into alignment. Experience comes first but it is possible for the mind to follow and for the two to operate together. Healthy religion promotes that alignment. Unhealthy religion encourages one to deal with secular and religious things as though they were different. They are the same. The Spirit is encountered in everything. The secular is also holy. To experience life that way is to be a mystic."

"Like you, Flying Eagle, I believe that all things are holy but I don't experience it that way much of the time. Why is that?"

"It is because you do not understand how to recognize the holy. You associate holiness with a particular feeling of mystery or awe or excitement or peace. You feel religious when you have particular feelings that you associate with an encounter with the holy. But the holy is not encountered on the level of feelings. The holy is encountered on the level of being. You must learn to recognize the holy with your being rather than with you feelings. Feelings, as important as they are, do not come from the being level. Feelings are an indicator that a shift is occurring. Feelings respond to energy flow. They are not an accurate indicator of states of being. People who love deeply do not go around feeling love all the time. They simply are love. Their actions express love and their presence exudes love but they may not feel love. If they start to love something that they have not loved before they may feel love but the feeling is an indicator that an energy shift is occurring as they start to love something new. If they continue to love that new thing, the feeling will usually subside and they will no longer feel love because they will have become love for that thing. Beware of people who operate out of their feelings rather than their being. They are not dependable. They require constant changes in order to produce feelings. Does this make sense to you?"

"Yes. But I must say that it is different from the way I have understood feelings in the past."

"What I am telling you now, Christians could have learned from the Stoics. Stoics were not opposed to having feelings. But they understood that feelings are not the same as being and that one should live out of the constancy of their being rather than out of their feelings. When a constant state of being is reached one does not feel that state.

"Now back to The Greatest Good. Your feelings may help you to identify The Greatest Good and you may have certain feelings as you start to live out The Greatest Good; but, if you continue along that path, you will not continue to have those feelings. The purpose is to be The Greatest Good, to express The Greatest Good, to live out The Greatest Good, rather than to feel The Greatest Good. Is that clear?"

"Yes, it is. So when I am following The Greatest Good for me and am teaching my students to experience the Spirit, I might not have any special feelings at all."

"That is correct. You will simply be yourself. The true you is not experienced as a feeling. The true you is a state of being."

❧ 17 ❧

I had been on the trail for over an hour when the sun came up. It had been a pleasant walk. Part of the time I had enjoyed following the trail with my eyes closed. For the last 20 minutes I had opened them and navigated by the predawn light so I could think. I wasn't quite sure why I was there. I had awakened during the night and followed an urge to go for a walk in the forest.

As I rounded a bend in the trail, I could see someone perhaps a hundred and fifty yards ahead of me. As I approached, something seemed familiar about the motionless figure, but I wasn't sure what it was. The man had long hair and wore traditional Indian buckskins.

"I have been waiting for you," he said.

His voice was beautiful–strong and powerful but also strangely tender. I had heard that voice once before. It was Star Man's.

"I am here to teach you about yourself," he continued. "You are about to pursue the Path of the Inner Journey in earnest. There are things that you must know to stay out of danger.

"Some pursue the Inner Journey and learn only about themselves. Others discover great truths concerning the Spirit as well. In order to learn about the Spirit on the journey, you must know that the Spirit dwells within you. As you discover your own inner nature you will discover the nature of the Spirit. The two are not the same but they are one. As you find yourself, you will find the Spirit. As you understand yourself, you will understand the Spirit. And as you discover the mystery of yourself, you will learn the true nature of the mystery of the Spirit. But you must understand that you are not the Spirit even though you are one with the Spirit. You are part of the whole but you are not the whole. In finding yourself, you will discover that the Spirit is in all of life and that the circumstances that you encounter are all of your own making and yet are in line with the will of the Spirit. Circumstances are not just the way the Spirit acts; your will, being one with the Spirit's will, also finds its expression in circumstances. Nothing is truly by accident.

Nothing happens without will behind it. The circumstances in your life are created by you. You create your own reality."

He suddenly disappeared. I was alone again in the forest.

The whole encounter seemed strange. What he had said seemed important and it made sense to me but it also seemed like something Flying Eagle could have and probably would have told me. Why did Star Man himself appear in order to give me that message? I wondered about it as I followed the trail back to the village.

I found Flying Eagle and told him I needed to talk to him.

"I had a strange experience this morning," I began, and then told him in detail about my encounter with Star Man.

"So what's the problem?" he asked.

"The problem is that the things he told me are things you could have told me. Why was there a special appearance of Star Man to convey information that you could have conveyed?"

"You, my friend, have missed the point of the encounter. The heart of his message to you is that you create your own reality. If you really understood his message you would be asking yourself why you created an appearance of Star Man to tell you that."

"But he was real. I didn't imagine him."

"Of course he was real. You still seem to think that you don't create reality. What you create is real. You can't create what is not real. It is real because you created it and you created it because it is real."

"I don't understand."

"You are having trouble understanding because you do not accept what Star Man told you. He told you that you create your own reality. He also said that you are one with the Spirit. Put the two principles together and see what you come up with. Then we will talk again."

He stood up and walked away.

All the next day I pondered about the visitation from Star Man and my subsequent talk with Flying Eagle. What was the connection between being one with the Spirit and creating my own reality? The two principles tumbled over and over in my brain. Finally they came together and I understood what Flying Eagle was trying to show me. I am one with the Spirit so what I create is also the Spirit's creation. It is the will of the Spirit for me to experience life the way it is. I create it but whatever I create is in accordance with the will of the Spirit because the Spirit wills that I create an experience of life that reflects my own inner nature. The meaning of life is not in the circumstances but in the growth that occurs from encountering the circumstances. Everything that I create is in one way or another a reflection of myself and everything that I create is in my life to be experienced. The Path of the Inner Journey is the process of discovering my will in everything that is and the Spirit's will in everything that is. Things are the way they are because I will them to be the way they are and things are the way they are because the Spirit wills them to be the way they are. The two are one.

I went back to Flying Eagle and told him what I had been thinking.

"Good," he said. "Now you understand."

"But I am not sure that I do understand. That view of reality creates as many theological problems for me as it solves. That view makes the evil that is in the world the will of the Spirit."

"Of course it is."

"But how can a God of love create evil?"

"The purpose of evil in the world is to show you yourself. The evil that you experience in the world is the evil that is within you. The Spirit wants you to encounter that evil and create a world that is good. That process of transforming the world will move no faster than the process of transforming yourself because you create expressions of yourself."

"But doesn't that make all of what I call reality simply an illusion, a projection of my own thoughts?"

"We are back to that question again. The answer is, 'No.' Reality is not an illusion. What you create is real. The fact that it is an expression of your own being does not make it any less real. The real world is real. Reality is not just a figment of your own imagination, but it is a product of your own state of being. Reality is what you have created. The evil in the world comes from within you. Your job is to encounter reality, to live in the real world, to encounter yourself; and when you encounter yourself in the evil you see in the world, your job is to transform the world into what your religion calls the Kingdom of God."

"I find this all very confusing."

"I know. That's why you created an encounter with Star Man. You needed him to reveal these principles to you first. If I had told you the way things are you would have thought that the confusion lay in how I was explaining it. The confusion does not lie there. The confusion lies within you."

"Let me see if I can put this all together. What I would call the Outward Journey and the Inner Journey are the same. The reality of the world around me is created by me and is an expression of my own inner state. When I change my inner state, the world changes. When I change the world, my inner state changes. Have I got that right?"

"Yes."

"I understand, but I'm still confused."

"I know. And you will remain confused until you change the nature of reality."

"What do you mean?"

"You will remain confused until you change the way your life works, change the way the world works, and change the way the universe works."

"Now wait a minute! Things are getting out of hand here. Change the Universe? You are making me sound like God."

"You still don't understand, do you? You and God are one. You and God create. You and God decide the nature of reality. And you and God decide how the universe will work for you."

"But I don't want to be making decisions that affect other people's lives in that way."

"Your decisions about how the Universe will work affect only you. That is the mystery of it all. Your reality does not affect other people's reality. It is your relationship with the Universe that we are talking about. Your experience of reality and another person's experience of reality can be quite different, even when encountering the same external events. I am not talking about changing other people's experience of reality. I am talking only about changing yours. The only way to change other people's experience of reality is by convincing them to change it for themselves. As you follow your calling to be a teacher, do not try to change your students. Merely share your understandings and give them the tools. Tell them that reality can be different. The students must decide whether or not to use the tools and whether or not to change reality for themselves. Your reality will not become your student's reality unless they choose it."

"Flying Eagle, I get the feeling that we are talking about two different levels of reality here. When you told me to change the way the Universe works I thought you meant that I was supposed to change the laws that affect matter in such a way that physical events would occur in a different way. You are talking about changing the way the Universe is experienced rather than the ways it works physically, aren't you."

"No, I am talking about both. When you change the way you experience the Universe, events will happen in a different way. Circumstances will start occurring in line with the way you experience the universe. Circumstances always conform to your experience of reality. If you don't like the way circumstances are occurring in your life, change your experience of reality and circumstances will occur in a different way. Circumstances occur in accordance with your will and the will of the Spirit. You create reality, remember?"

"Yes. I think I am starting to understand in a new way what you told me before."

"Good. Maybe now you will change the way the Universe works for you. That is what Star Man was leading up to. You created an appearance of Star Man to help you get over this hurdle. The Inner Journey will lead you into a new reality. That is its purpose. The Inner Journey does not just change you. It changes the Universe. Some think that the Inner Journey is just a journey into new understandings of oneself. The true Inner Journey also leads to a new experience of the Spirit and a new experience of reality."

✣ 18 ✣

The next three days were largely taken up with driving and work for the college. I left the village and drove for hours to interview two of the candidates for the opening in the religion department. I returned to the village the evening of the third day. I was tired and frustrated.

"How was your trip?" Flying Eagle asked when he saw me.

"Very disappointing. Both candidates were interesting and both had an excellent grasp of religion intellectually, but they had little grasp of what it really means to live in relation to the Spirit. They were unacceptable. I can't expect students to learn how to value their experience of the Spirit if their professors haven't experienced what they are teaching about."

"The candidates and the interviews are your creation. They reflect your inner being. What did they teach you about yourself?"

"What do you mean?"

"You still have not grasped it, have you? You created an appearance of Star Man in part to tell you that you create your own reality. You asked me about the subject and I have been telling you about it as well. You understand intellectually what we told you. But when it comes to making that understanding a part of your life and living out what it means to create your own reality, you are confused. What went into your head did not get down to your heart. Don't you think it interesting that each of the two people you created to interview for the position also has difficulty getting head and heart together?"

"You are saying that their problem is the same as mine?"

"Yes. In a sense you were interviewing yourself. Until you deal with that issue within yourself, you are very likely to find that everyone you interview is unable to get head and heart together. You created them and, because you created them, they are going to be a lot like you. You created them in your own image.

"Look to find yourself in the world around you. When you get your head and your heart together you will see reflections of yourself in everything that you create and you will find the Spirit in everything you create as well."

"I am more comfortable with the thought that I created the interviews than I am with the thought that I also created the people I interviewed. Are you telling me that they would not have existed if I had not created them?"

"They would not have existed in your reality unless you had created them.

"Creation is not what you think it is. You are starting to grasp that the Spirit creates and that you, too, create, but you do not yet comprehend that your creation and the Spirit's creation are the same. You are uncomfortable with the idea of creating people because you associate that action only with the Spirit. The Spirit is part of you and you are part of the Spirit.

"Anything that is beyond your realm of reality is for you as though it does not exist. When you create, things or people come into your realm of reality that did not exist *for you* before. The people you created were not in your realm of reality until you created them. The question of whether or not they existed before you created them does not make sense. As far as your reality is concerned they did not exist. Nothing exists in your reality that you have not created. Nothing exists in your reality that the Spirit has not created. If you choose to move into another realm of reality, other things may exist for you there but what is not in your current realm of reality does not currently exist for you."

"Do other things exist for the Spirit that are not part of my own reality?"

"If I said yes, I would be telling a lie. But if I said no, I would not be speaking the truth. This is part of the mystery of the Spirit. Reality is determined by your realm of reality. The Spirit chooses to operate within your realm of reality most of the time. When the Spirit is operating within your reality nothing exists that is not within your reality. When the Spirit chooses to bring things from outside your reality into your reality then they do exist but only when they come into your reality. Do you understand the problem? How can I tell you that something is real that is not real in your reality? All I can say is that what is real for me is not the same as what is real for you."

Having said that he held up his hand indicating that the discussion was over. He headed back to his lodge. I went back to my room, pondered what he and Star Man had told me about reality, and went to sleep.

❧ 19 ❧

When I awakened, it was morning. I felt refreshed. The past three days of driving and interviewing felt far behind me. It was good to be back in familiar surroundings and among the people of the village.

It was a beautiful day. The sun was shining brightly, the air was crystal clear and the temperature was just right. It felt good to be alive.

The forest beckoned.

I had been on the trail for about fifteen minutes when I felt an urge to sit and meditate. I saw a log near the trail and sat down.

Time passed. The silence felt profound. I was aware only of an abiding sense of joy and inner peace. Hours went by; I did not know how many and I did not care. There was something different about this period of meditation. Usually my mind would have thoughts or memories running through it nearly constantly when I sat in silence. Today there were long gaps of nothingness when I just *was*, with no thoughts, no memories, just a silent sense of oneness with myself and with the Universe. I was aware that I was being fed by the silence. It was meeting a deep inner craving and need. I had no significant thoughts, no insights, no visions or mystical experiences all day. There was just the silence, the wonderful silence.

I returned to the village late in the afternoon and found Flying Eagle sitting in front of his lodge, this time without a novel in his hands.

"I have been waiting for you," he said as I approached. "I could sense something was happening deep within your spirit today and I thought you would want to talk about it."

"I do. That's why I came looking for you, but I don't know what to say. I spent the day in the forest meditating in silence. There were long periods when my thoughts stopped and I just *was*. I feel different, but I don't understand what happened or how I have changed."

"You are now on the Path of Silence."

"I realize that, Flying Eagle, but what happened to the Path of the Inner Journey? I was just starting to work on that one."

"The Inner Journey will continue. The paths are not to be followed one at a time. The Paths are to be added in a particular order, but you must not abandon the previous Paths when a new one is added. They are to be followed simultaneously. When you started the Path of the Inner Journey it opened you to experience the Path of Silence on a deeper level, but that does not mean that you no longer need to work on deep issues within yourself. The journey along each path must be continued or your growth will stop and you will not experience the full Power of Circumstance in your life.

"As I said, the order in which you follow The Paths is very important. Each path opens the way for the next path. The Greatest Good opens the way for the Inner Journey, which in turn opens the way for Silence. You are starting the Path of Silence but the Path of the Greatest Good and the Path of the Inner Journey must be continued."

"Can you tell me more about the Path of Silence."

"There is little that I can say. The silence must be experienced. As you have already discovered, it can not be understood."

"But what happened to me? Something changed in me and I don't know what it was or how it happened."

"In the deep silence one is in tune with the Spirit. The unity between your spirit and the Great Spirit is experienced and strengthened but it is not experienced on the level of thought nor is it usually encountered on the level of feeling. The power of the silence is encountered on a level that is deeper than thoughts or feelings. The only things that you might regularly sense as you enter into the silence are that you are at peace and that you are being fed within."

"I did feel my soul being fed but I also seem to have been changed."

"You have been changed. Not only has your spirit been strengthened but a new area within yourself has experienced growth in your Inner Journey."

"Which area?"

"I can not tell you but I will show you."

He went inside his lodge. A moment later he was standing in the doorway holding a large hunting knife. He let out a loud scream and charged at me with the knife.

"I'm going to kill you!" he shouted and plunged the knife toward my heart.

The blade stopped its forward motion at the last instant. I looked down. The point of the blade was touching my shirt right in front of my heart.

"You did not move," he said, breaking into a wide grin.

He was right. I realized with some amazement that my hands were still at my sides.

"Why did you not move to protect yourself?"

"I don't know."

You are trusting your inner awareness now and following it instead of your instincts. Your inner awareness told you that you would not die. Your instincts would have told you to protect yourself. When one follows the Path of Silence one's inner awareness is deepened and it can affect one's actions. That has happened to you. But it will not last unless you continue to practice silence. Continue to follow the Path and other changes will unfold that will complement your Inner Journey.

"But why did that change?"

"What do you mean, 'why'? I just told you. The silence brought the change."

"I understand that. What I mean is, why does the silence have that affect on me? I expect things to change in me when I work on them. I don't expect things within to change when I am not working on inner issues."

"You are too much a product of your society, Screaming Hawk. You expect everything to come about through your own efforts.

"In the realm of the Spirit much occurs that is not the result of one's own efforts. There are many things one can not change about oneself regardless of the amount of effort put forth. But when one experiences the oneness that already exists with the Spirit, the Spirit quite often responds by bringing forth inner changes in the person. The Spirit enjoys giving gifts. In your religion it is called 'grace.'

"The silence is important because it opens you to receive gifts. But remember, it is the Spirit who chooses what those gifts to you will be. You can not control them. If you had entered into the silence today in order to strengthen your inner awareness, it would not have happened. The gifts are gifts. They should not be requested from the Spirit. Always enter into the silence without an agenda, without asking for anything. The Spirit will decide what to give and when to give it.

"Many times the Spirit chooses to give no gift at all; but that, in itself, is a gift, for that keeps the silence pure. If the Spirit always gave you a gift in the silence, then entering the silence would become another way to earn things through your own efforts.

"Live life as though your own efforts and insights are important, or to put it another way, follow the Inner Journey, but also live out of the awareness that there is much that comes to you that is not earned. Leave room for gifts in your life. Those who think that everything depends on their own efforts hamper their own growth. The Spirit loves to give. But the Spirit gives the most to those who do not try to earn the Spirit's favor.

"I have told you as much as I can about the Path of Silence. Do not expect to understand it. Silence is experienced on a level deeper than understanding. But know this, it is extremely important to practice silence regularly. It will not only hasten your inner growth, it will also increase the Power of Circumstance in your life."

❧ 20 ❧

Each day I entered the forest for time alone in silence. I continued to have no strong feelings during the silence, but the sense that my soul was being fed continued. Subtle changes were occurring in my thoughts and reactions. I noticed I was becoming more patient, less quick to get angry when circumstances were not as I wanted. In one of our sessions Flying Eagle commented about the change he saw in me.

"Part of the reason you are not as angry, Screaming Hawk, is that you are starting to heal the many wounds of your childhood. People who get angry easily are usually people with many wounds. Their anger is a protection against further injury. The problem is that it also protects them from the experience of the healing pain."

"Healing pain? What do you mean?"

"Pain can be healing. It is important to learn how to experience pain in a way that brings life rather than further injury to an individual. Emotional pain is not to be feared or avoided. Pain is a gift from the Spirit and its presence can allow one to grow in ways that are not possible when life is easy. There are many sources of emotional pain but one of the most common sources is coming face to face with the lack of perfection that we seek outside of ourselves. We want our parents to be perfect. We want our lovers or spouses to be perfect. We want things that we own to be perfect. Many of us believe, on some level, that if we were just surrounded by enough perfection that our lives would become perfect. The anger that many people have at their parents stems from the mistaken belief that they themselves would not have to endure problems and emotional conflict if their parents had raised them perfectly.

"But perfection is not the absence of imperfections. It is the presence of imperfections around us that gives us life and stimulates growth. True perfection can be encountered only after we realize that everything is already exactly the way that it should be and that the entire Universe is in alignment to bring us wholeness and growth.

"Do not serve the Spirit because the Spirit is perfect. The Spirit will not give you perfection by making that which is around you be without blemish. The beauty of the Spirit is that perfection is given in the midst of brokenness. Brokenness is perfect. It amazes me that Christians have such difficulty understanding that concept. It is part of what the crucifixion was all about. Star Man, or Jesus, if you prefer, was broken when he hung on the cross. It was through his brokenness that transformation came. The Spirit gives you the pathway to wholeness by urging you to experience your own brokenness. Do not be confused by this. Perfection is not about being without blemish. Perfection is about being, being to the fullest, being all that you are, including your brokenness. The person who thinks he has to be without blemish in order to be acceptable has missed the whole point. To be perfect is to be your imperfect self to the fullest.

"The gift of perfection is given to us at creation but it lies unrecognized until we are able to fully recognize and accept our own brokenness. It is then that we discover that we were perfect all the time and that we had the perfect parents for us and that it is imperfection that makes life perfect.

"Pay close attention to what I am telling you, Screaming Hawk. You will never enter into the deepest realms of the Spirit until you stop trying to have everything, including yourself, be without blemish. Recognizing one's blemishes leads to perfection. Doing away with them does not. Do you understand?"

"Yes, I think so. But why is there so much focus on sin in Christianity if perfection already exists for us?"

"Because unless one recognizes one's own sinfulness, one's own imperfections, one can not take the next step and discover that even sin is part of one's own perfection."

"O.K. I understand, but it still seems strange to me that it is that way."

"Of course it seems strange. True perfection is strange to our natural way of thinking. Part of our imperfection is that we all look for perfection where it is not before we are capable of finding it where it truly is. But when we discover that imperfection is perfection, all of life and everything that *is* becomes strangely beautiful.

"Do not expect this teaching to become true for you through your understanding. You have understood what I have told you, but that is not enough. You must experience its truth. Only then will you be capable of fully experiencing the Spirit in everything that is and everything that happens. Only then will you be capable of finding healing in all of your pain and be able to experience it as a gift to you from the Spirit."

I continued to think about Flying Eagle's teaching about perfection but it was not until several days later that I experienced what he had been talking about. That day I had been sitting under a tree in the forest meditating in silence for some time. When I stood up to leave I somehow twisted my ankle and fell to the ground. The pain was excruciating. I swore out loud as I held my ankle and chastised myself for my own clumsiness.

Then suddenly it all seemed ironic. There I was swearing at the top of my lungs because I was feeling pain, pain that Flying Eagle said was a gift from the Spirit. I realized that I had always thought of pain as something bad, an indicator that something was wrong. What if pain is merely a useful message that something has changed? In the past I had thought of having a sprained ankle as bad and of having a painless ankle as good. Was there really a difference? On the surface the answer seemed to be "yes," but on a deeper level the answer seemed to be "no," that having a sprained ankle really was neither good nor bad. The pain could be viewed as merely an indicator that a change had occurred in my ankle and that, as a result, a change in the way I treated my ankle was appropriate.

I noticed when I tried to put my weight on my ankle that the pain increased. If I took my weight off the ankle the pain lessened. The pain was useful in discovering what changes I needed to make. I merely needed to change the way I walked for a while.

Could emotional pain be viewed in the same way, as a message from the Spirit that something has changed and that I might need to deal with my circumstances in a different way? The thought intrigued me. I realized that when I think of pain as bad or a sign that something is wrong, my first impulse is to try to change the circumstances. But when I think of pain as a sign only that something has changed, my first response is not to change the circumstances but to change the way I relate to the circumstances.

I was no longer feeling angry about my injury. It had become an opportunity for insight. It was now a gift from the Spirit.

I picked up a nearby limb that was sturdy enough to use as a walking stick, stood up and managed to maneuver my way back to the village without putting weight on my injured ankle. Since I was now walking in a different way, my ankle did not bother me.

Later that day I saw Flying Eagle and talked to him about my insight regarding pain.

"Your understanding is basically correct," he said. "One of the ways the Spirit uses pain is to show us that a change has occurred and that we may need to mobilize our inner resources to deal with life differently. You did that on two levels with your ankle. You reorganized your thinking about pain and you also changed the way you were walking. But pain is also an opportunity to reorganize one's awareness of the nature of reality. Things are not the way they appear and life is not the way it appears. Life looks different when people are experiencing pain; their values shift and they make decisions in a different way.

"Physical injuries or illnesses provide opportunities to learn new ways to get along in life. Because of the injury to your ankle you have had to learn a new way to walk. Sometimes the spirit uses a physcial disorder to teach a self-reliant person how to depend on others to meet their needs. Growth occurs when we learn new ways to deal with life. Many people have grown faster with a physical disability than they did before they developed their physical limitation. You may have met people who have had that experience. Your culture tends to view all physical limitations as bad. They are not. The purpose of life is to grow inwardly. Having physical limitations can be a real asset to growth for some people and people with physical limitations should never be looked upon as being unfortunate."

"But doesn't that way of thinking about physical limitations lead to a lack of concern about curing people's injuries or illnesses?"

"No. It is not wrong to cure an injury or an illness. The problem is that doctors often help people get well physically but do nothing to help their patients grow inwardly. Then the illness becomes a waste and the pain that the person has endured is meaningless. There is no illness or pain that can not be meaningful. The Spirit is present in all things and all experiences can produce growth. If someone is ill he should learn from his illness first and then recover if he likes.

"When a person is ill or injured, he is imperfect. But even illness, even physical imperfection, is perfect and can produce inner growth. One should not ignore the opportunity for growth that illnesses and injuries provide.

"Your ankle is sprained. Recover from it if you like. But let your ankle teach you in the meantime."

❧ 21 ❧

My time alone in the forest had become more and more important to me. I was pleased that I could find meaning merely in being present in the silence. I felt good about the progress I was making. But my contentment was to be short lived.

The next day after I had been sitting alone in the forest for a couple of hours meditating in silence and minding my own business, the hawk appeared. Although I had not consciously called for him, he swooped down and landed a few feet in front of me. I was both surprised and pleased to see him. Unlike most previous occasions, he spoke to me almost immediately.

"You need help," he said. "You need a lot of help."

"Oh?" I responded, bristling slightly in response to the condescending tone in his voice.

"Yes. You need help and I am here to straighten you out."

He paced back and forth for a minute like some sort of feathered executive collecting his thoughts in the midst of dictating an important letter.

"You," he continued, "think you have some sort of inside track on the Spirit. You don't. All this time you are spending in the forest meditating is getting in the way of your progress. It's time someone told you, and I am here to do exactly that."

"What do you mean?"

"There you go opening your mouth again. If you will just keep your mouth shut and listen, I will explain what I mean so that even someone like you can understand."

I was not quite sure whether to laugh or feel insulted but I kept my mouth shut.

"Your training needs some practical direction at this point. You are in danger of becoming one of those religious eggheads who sits around spouting religious-sounding spiritual nonsense and collecting followers around him who want to 'know the Spirit' or 'meditate on the mysteries' or some sort of crap like that. You are starting to lose touch with reality and to think that life is about sitting in silence and twiddling your thumbs until the Spirit speaks to your soul.

"Now don't get me wrong. Silence is important and those who don't practice it are missing out on an important part of the process of spiritual growth. But those who practice too much silence can lose their perspective and become mystics who have lost touch with the real world around them. You, my friend, are in danger of doing exactly that. These trips into the forest to meditate are getting out of hand. You need some balance in your life. When was the last time you had a beer with the boys or went to a ball game or cut the grass or did any of those other rituals that are so much a part of your culture? Are you afraid of experiencing life? You think the Spirit can be found here in the forest, don't you? You think that to turn inward and meditate in silence is the way to be a spiritual being, don't you? It is, but it isn't. Flying Eagle has told you that it is and he is right. But I'm here to tell you that it isn't and I, of course, am even more right.

"Now wait a minute! I saw you starting to open your mouth again. You were about to speak again; weren't you? You were about to open that big ugly mouth of yours and make some comment or ask another one of your asinine questions."

I closed my mouth.

"Good. That's better.

"Now, as I was saying, you are losing all of your perspective. It is not the Spirit's intent that you totally separate yourself from the world in which you live. Mystics who do that are, as you say, a dime a dozen and that's all they are worth. Balance is what the spirit is interested in and it is balance that you don't have right now. So listen to me and get yourself out of the forest more and into the real world or you will become a real spiritual pain in the ass. Have you got that?"

I nodded my head.

"Good."

He turned and flew off.

I sat in stunned silence for a few moments absorbing what he had said. Then I stood up and headed back to the village.

The next day I told Flying Eagle about my encounter with the hawk.

He chuckled.

"That bird is good for you," he said. "And he is right. You have been putting too much focus on the spiritual Paths lately. You need to relax. You are too intense. You need to regain your perspective. I think it would be good for you to go have a few beers with the boys. Meditation should not be an escape from life. It should put you in touch with life and give you a deeper appreciation for everything. Those who use meditation as an escape fail to learn the most important principle of all, that the Spirit is everywhere and in everything. You do not have balance unless you can find the Spirit in the midst of a ball game or an evening with the boys.

"I'll see you on Tuesday. I'm sending you on a secular retreat. Get out of here. Go to the city and regain your balance. And if you spend any time meditating I will take that knife of mine and cut you into little pieces and feed you to that bird of yours."

❧ 22 ❧

I followed orders. I drove to the city.

Over the next three days I went to three ball games, ate peanuts and yelled my head off; saw all the movies worth seeing; read half of a science fiction thriller and even had "a few beers with the boys". The latter was the only unpleasant part of my mini-vacation.

The bar I had selected looked innocent enough and was in a good location, still in the business district but not very far from some nice residential areas. I expected it to be a watering hole for young executives on their way home from the office. As I entered, I fully expected the place to be filled with people in coats and ties and wondered if my neat, but casual, attire would be appropriate. To my surprise, I was definitely over dressed for the place. Blue jeans, "T" shirts; some faded, some smeared with grease; and, even a few cowboy boots were in vogue there. The place was filled with off duty truckers. My first impulse was to leave immediately, but I decided to stay when it occurred to me that it might be "interesting" to watch the truckers interact with each other for a while.

I took a seat at a table near the bar, ordered a beer and sat back to watch and to listen. At the table closest to me the men were talking about trucks. At another, three men were swapping tails, in rather graphic terms, about their exploits with women. From somewhere else in the room there were occasional bursts of laughter, apparently in response to some joke or funny story someone was telling.

I felt out of place and ill at ease. And very quickly I became bored as well. I was debating about leaving when my attention was drawn to a belligerent looking man who was sitting by himself at the bar. I heard him mutter insulting comments in the direction of the bartender every time he moved out of earshot. At one point the man spilled his beer. The bartender came over and mopped it up with a rag. When the man ordered another beer, the bartender told him politely that he had had enough.

The man became insistent. The bartender explained that it was against the law for him to serve anyone who was intoxicated. The man then started shouting insults and making threats.

At that point one of the customers, a large man with a goatee who was more than six feet tall and well over 270 pounds, stood up and came over to the man at the bar. "My name is George," he said politely. "You seem to be upset. Can I help?"

Without warning the man whirled around and took a swing at George. George easily blocked the blow with one of his massive arms, spun the man around, picking him up under both arms, carried him out of the bar.

One of the customers yelled, "Yeah George!" Someone else applauded. Then the customers returned to their conversations as though nothing had happened.

I was frightened. My heart was pounding. I quickly paid my bill and left the bar.

❧ 23 ❧

"How did it go?" Flying Eagle asked when I saw him again.

I told him about my time away, about going to the movies and the ball games, and finally, in detail, about my experience in the bar.

"What scared you in the bar, Screaming Hawk?"

"The violence."

"No, Screaming Hawk, before that. Something scared you."

"I wasn't scared before the man at the bar started shouting."

Flying Eagle looked unconvinced. "Who did you talk to in the bar?"

"Nobody."

"Nobody?"

"Yes. Nobody."

"Don't you think it strange that you didn't talk to anybody in that bar? I suspect that everyone else in there had a conversation with somebody. Even the hostile man at the bar had an interaction with the bar tender."

"I just wanted to watch and listen."

"So you said. What scared you?"

"Why do you keep asking that?"

"Because you haven't really answered my question. I know you pretty well, Screaming Hawk. When you are scared you get passive. You may have felt your fear consciously when the violence started to break out but that was not what scared you; you were afraid long before that. That's why you chose to be a passive observer."

He placed a hand on my shoulder. "Screaming Hawk, are you scared of life?"

"What do you mean?"

"The fear of life," he responded, "is not always experienced through one's feelings. Sometimes that fear is demonstrated in withdrawal or passivity. In your culture, there are many who are afraid of life, people who observe life without truly living it. Those truckers scare you because they are in touch with life in a way that you are not. You judge them to be beneath you because many of them are not well educated. But they are in touch with life and there is much that you could learn if you chose to interact with them. But you, my friend, became frightened and decided to watch instead. That's what you do with the Spirit also. You, like many others, enter The Silence to watch the Spirit. When one watches the Spirit one sees only oneself. The Spirit is there to be encountered, not to be watched, and life is there to be lived. The Spirit is encountered in the midst of life. You don't fully understand that yet but many of those truckers do. They have much to teach you, Screaming Hawk."

Flying Eagle paused as if to put special emphasis on what he was about to ask next. "And what did you do after you left the bar?"

"Well, it took me a while to calm down. I took a walk and then went back to my motel room and meditated."

"You meditated?"

"Yes."

"Screaming Hawk, I gave you strict orders not to meditate while you were away. Don't you remember, I told you that I would cut you into little pieces and feed you to that hawk if you did?"

"Well yes. But I thought you were kidding."

"I was not serious about cutting you into pieces but I was absolutely serious about the importance of your not meditating while you were away. Screaming Hawk, you still don't understand do you? Lately you have been using meditation to escape from life. You were more fully in contact with the Spirit in that bar than you have been for weeks. That's what scared you!"

"I don't understand."

"I know."

He sighed and walked away.

❧ 24 ❧

The next day Flying Eagle invited me to join him on a walk in the forest.

"Have you been thinking any more about your experience in the bar?" he asked, as we headed down one of the trails.

"Yes. But I'm still confused."

"What is confusing you?"

"Everything. You seem to put a lot of importance on what happened to me in that bar."

"Yes, I do."

"Why?"

"Because there is much for you to learn from that experience.

"Screaming Hawk, part of what is confusing you is that you have misunderstood the purpose of mediation. Many people assume that the Spirit is most powerfully encountered away from the distractions of daily life. Through meditation, those people seek to free themselves of distractions and have a pure encounter with the Spirit. But the Spirit is not encountered in the absence of distractions, Screaming Hawk; the Spirit is most powerfully encountered in the midst of the distractions of life.

"You were afraid of an encounter with the Spirit in the midst of life, so you withdrew from life and became a passive observer in that bar. You also succeeded in withdrawing from your feelings. That's why you did not feel your fear at first. But when the man at the bar started creating a disturbance, you became somewhat distracted, and when he was having the physical confrontation with George, you were totally distracted by the events. You were in touch with life. You had an encounter with the Spirit and it terrified you. It was not the violence that scared you, Screaming Hawk. It was the Spirit that scared you. To live life in a direct encounter with the Spirit can be terrifying. And we encounter the Spirit most fully when we are fully distracted by life, when we are fully living life. That's what happened to you in the bar.

"The purpose of meditation is not to remove oneself from the distractions of life but to prepare oneself to encounter the Spirit in the midst of life. The power of meditation is that meditation itself becomes such a big distraction that contact with the Spirit is made. Now you know what many others do not understand. Use that knowledge well. It will make your path much easier.

"You have been a prisoner of your own misconceptions and prejudices about people and about the Spirit. You missed the richness of the opportunity that was available to you in that bar. Although many truck drivers use profanity and do not use terms that most people associate with the Spirit, many of them are profoundly spiritual people. Don't be deceived. If you listen between their words, you may hear things that will astound you.

"That bar is an excellent place for you to learn more about the Spirit. The Spirit is everywhere.

"In the past you have encountered the Spirit while meditating here in the forest, but that doesn't mean that you must go to the forest to encounter the Spirit. The Spirit is everywhere. The Spirit is in that bar. The Spirit is in the distractions of life."

"But didn't Jesus go off alone at times to pray?"

"Yes, and at times I would recommend that you do the same. But it was not that he was unable to encounter the Spirit when he was with people. In fact, it was the common people whom he seemed to enjoy the most and it was the common people to whom he aimed most of his teachings. Look closely at his style of teaching. Many of his images are from the life experiences of farmers, shepherds and fishermen. They heard his message and responded to it. Often the common people, such as truck drivers, are more in touch with life than the intellectuals. Being in touch with life makes one open to the Spirit. It is easy for a college professor, like you, to think that intellect is important for the life of the Spirit. It is not. Being in touch with the reality of life is much more important and it is that quality of being in touch with reality that makes the common people particularly open to the Spirit. When you learn how to talk to truck drivers about the life of the Spirit, without using theological language, you will be ready to teach your students how to encounter the Spirit without interference from their intellect. In the meantime, know that you missed an important opportunity to learn about the Spirit from those truck drivers.

"Screaming Hawk, one of the secrets of the Universe is that the Spirit is most powerfully found where one is not looking. The Spirit delights in that. People's attempts to control the Spirit don't work. Most of the religious experiences of your people do not occur at church and my people rarely have their most important religious experiences at our rituals. The ceremonies have value but their true value, like meditation, is to prepare people to encounter the Spirit in the midst of the distractions of life. Remember that. It will simplify your search tremendously."

❦ 25 ❦

Finding balance was not easy. I repeatedly fell back into my old pattern of expecting the Spirit to be where I was looking and I continued to find it difficult to be open to encountering the Spirit in the midst of life. On three more occasions Flying Eagle sent me back to the bar to converse with the truck drivers and to find the Spirit in their midst. Each trip was a dismal failure. Each time I had to report back that I had not encountered the Spirit among the people in the bar. Each time he said, "Then we will work some more and try again."

I was getting frustrated. Every few days I was spending hours driving to and from the city to spend a few hours sitting in a third-rate bar listening to truck drivers talk about ball games and trucks and women. Nothing they said seemed profound. Nothing they said led me to believe they had any interest in the Spirit.

"What is it that I am supposed to be getting out of all this?"

I had asked Flying Eagle that question repeatedly over the past days. Each time he had ignored my question or given me an evasive answer. But finally he answered me directly.

"Nothing."

"What?"

"Nothing. That is what you are supposed to get. Nothing."

"I don't understand."

"Of course you don't understand. That is exactly the point. You keep trying to understand. You keep looking for depth with your mind. You keep thinking that you are going to encounter the Spirit through your intellect. But you don't and you won't. The truck drivers know that. You don't. I sent you there to learn from the truck drivers but the skull protecting your pea-sized brain is so thick that the truth has continued to elude you.

"Did you notice that the truck drivers were totally uninterested in talking to you about theories?"

"Yes I did. And I found it very frustrating."

"Did you notice that even in their coarse talk about women and sex that their total focus was on experience?"

"Yes. But most of them were talking about women as though they were mere sex objects. Surely you don't approve of that."

"Of course not, but I did not send you there to learn about sex or about women. I sent you there to learn about the Spirit. They all know that the most important thing about life or sex or the Spirit is to experience it, not to understand it. You, my friend, are still afraid of the life force. Those truckers are in touch with it and that is why they scare the Hell out of you. You would rather understand life than live it. You would rather understand the Spirit than encounter it. Would you also rather understand sex than experience it?"

"No. In that third category I am definitely dedicated to the value of experience."

"Well good! At least we can be thankful for that!" he said with a little chuckle. He paused for a moment and then turned serious again. "So, if you can approach sex as though the experience is of primary importance, why is it that you have so much trouble doing the same with life and with the Spirit?"

"I'm not sure," I said honestly.

"I will tell you why. You are still scared. You are scared of life and you are scared of the Spirit. And until you face that fact, you are going to continue to run from life and the Spirit while deluding yourself into thinking that your desire to understand is a sign of your openness."

"You might be right, Flying Eagle. But if you are right, what do I do about it?"

"You go back to your Inner Journey. You must search deep within yourself and confront your fear. Many qualities are needed to pursue the spiritual journey but, of them all, courage is the most important. You must confront your fear. We can not proceed until you have done that."

26

Knowing that my block to further growth was fear had not seemed to help. I had thought about it. I had meditated about it. I had written about it in my journal. Nothing seemed to help. Flying Eagle was still refusing to talk to me until I encountered my fear, and repeated attempts to call on my power animal for assistance had yielded nothing. The hawk had come once but had flown right past me as if to demonstrate that he was avoiding me also, until I had dealt with my fear.

I was feeling desperate. My Inner Journey was at a standstill and the summer was slipping away. It would soon be time to return to the college.

Finally, I went to Flying Eagle and told him that I had decided to return to the bar one more time and talk to a truck driver about my situation.

"Good. It's about time," he said and sent me on my way.

When I walked into the place, there was only one customer, a large man wearing his usual dungarees and faded "T" shirt. Even though his back was turned to me, I recognized him at once. It was George. I had a sinking feeling in the pit of my stomach. Of all the people who frequented the bar he was the last one I would have chosen to talk to about my situation.

I ordered a beer and stood at the bar for a few minutes hoping someone else would come in. No one did.

I thought about leaving but the thought of driving all those miles back to the reservation without accomplishing my mission and then trying to explain it to Flying Eagle was too much. Finally, I walked over to the booth where George was sitting.

"Mind if I sit down?" I asked nervously.

"Nope. I have been waiting for you."

I sat down across from him.

"What do you mean you have been waiting for me?"

"I knew you would be coming back here today and I knew that you needed to talk to someone about the Spirit. That's why I'm here."

"How did you know that?"

"If I told you, you would laugh." He paused and looked at me long and hard. "Then again, maybe you wouldn't. How much do you already know about the Spirit?"

"More than most, I suppose. I've been studying under Flying Eagle for the past two summers."

"I've heard of him. He's some sort of a medicine man up on the reservation, isn't he?"

"Yes."

"I've never met him. Some say he has unusual powers. Others say he's a quack. I figure he's probably for real, but I don't know."

"He's for real," I said, unconsciously slipping into George's vernacular.

"In that case," George responded, "the things I have to tell you might not seem strange to you. Anybody who has studied under a real medicine man has to have a pretty open mind.

"I was hauling a load back from Tucson Thursday when I saw him hitchhiking out in the middle of nowhere."

"Him?"

"Him. I don't know his name. When I tell you who I think he is, you're gona think I'm nuts." He looked at me hard again, but only a moment this time. "Then again, maybe you won't.

"I've given him a ride three times before. The first time he was hitchhiking in the middle of a snow storm up on Berthoud Pass. I don't usually pick up riders, especially ones with long hair, but he looked pleasant enough, even with his long hair. He didn't look like a hippie or anybody weird like that. And he needed a ride bad, 'cause it was real cold. So I gave him a ride.

"He turned out to be the most interesting fella I've ever met. We talked half through the night about all sorts of things. He seemed to have a different slant on life. He was really into making the world work better and talked about being one with nature and other people and stuff like that, but what he said made sense, real sense. Then all of a sudden, he said we were where he wanted to get off. By that time we were in the middle of Nebraska. I mean, there wasn't anything around for miles, but that's where he said he wanted to get off, so I stopped on the side of the highway and let him off. I said to him, 'I don't even know your name.' And he said, 'They call me by many names. Since you don't seem to like hippies much, just think of me as an old hippie.' That's what he said. Then he took off his glove to shake my hand as he said goodbye. That's when I saw the wound in his hand. I started to ask him about it but he just climbed out of the cab and closed the door. I drove on. I was about thirty miles down the road before it hit me. 'My God!' I said. 'Was that Jesus?'"

He paused and looked straight at me again.

"I guess you've got to decide now who you think he was because the last time I picked him up, two days ago, he said you were going to be here and that there was a message I was supposed to give you, and that you would understand what it meant. He told me to tell you that he is 'an old truck driver.' Does that mean anything to you?"

"Yes, I think so," I said, feeling like a fool. It was then that I heard it. Someone was laughing. Someone spelled with a big 'S' was laughing and I laughed too.

❧ 27 ❧

"So what do you understand the meaning of that message to be? Flying Eagle interrupted, as I was telling him about my encounter with George."I think it means that I meet Jesus in the midst of my prejudices and I think that is what I am afraid of. I am scared that I am going to discover that the Spirit does not fit my image of the Spirit. I'm afraid the Spirit might really be active in somebody like George."

"*I* understand your words and their meaning, but I am not sure that *you* fully understand them yet, Screaming Hawk. It is one thing to speak the truth and quite another to experience the truth."

"George is the epitome of all my college professor prejudices against truck drivers. He is rough, uncultured, and his appearance makes me mildly nauseous. He is even prejudiced against those whom he calls hippies and I, as a well-educated, liberal-thinking, enlightened intellectual am profoundly prejudiced against people who are prejudiced. And if that weren't enough, George even resorts to physical violence. He scares me. He is the embodiment of all my prejudices. I am afraid to encounter the Spirit in George because I have created George to represent everything that I find beneath me. I created George to be, for me, where the Spirit *is not*, but he has become, for me, where the Spirit *is*. That is profoundly disturbing to me because I have just realized that what I truly fear, above all else, is the possibility that the Spirit is not only encountered in all the distractions of life but in the people who create those distractions as well. I want the Spirit to be under my control. I want to be able to decide where the Spirit is and where the Spirit is not. And if the Spirit can be encountered in George, the object of my prejudices, then the Spirit truly is beyond my control. That scares the daylights out of me.

"It was a long time in coming, Flying Eagle, but now I really do accept that, in one way or another, I and the Spirit work together to create everything that I experience. I help to create my own experience but I do not, in any way, create the Spirit. The Spirit just *is*."

Flying Eagle broke into a broad smile. "Tell me more about that," he said.

"I hadn't fully realized it before, but I think I always had a sneaking suspicion that I had created the Spirit in some way and that without me the Spirit would not exist. It sounds egocentric, but I really did suspect that. It was the issue of experience that brought that to light. I do not experience the Spirit in the same ways that I think about the Spirit. I can fantasize that the Spirit is this way or that way or that the Spirit does this or that, but when it comes right down to it, I encounter the Spirit in ways that do not fit my understanding. I can come to understand the actions of the Spirit afterwards but never beforehand. I know this is a paradox, but I have come to believe that although the Spirit and I create everything in my reality together, the Spirit also acts totally independently of me. It is that independence that terrifies me, because it means that I am not in control of what happens even though I have created it."

"You have done well, Screaming Hawk. That truth does not come easily to people. We have a need to control the Spirit so much that, at times, we delude ourselves into thinking that we do not have control of anything. That is where the notion that the Spirit creates everything and that we have no say about any of it comes from. Our need for control is so great that we pretend that we do not have any control. That is where the role of victim, that so many people play, comes from. The victim of life is the person who is still pretending that he or she does not have a desperate need to control everything. The irony is that we do control everything within our experience, everything except the Spirit. But the victim does not understand that. The victim, despite all appearances to the contrary, is actually trying to control the Spirit. By pretending not to be in control of anything, the victim, is in fact, trying to control everything, including the Spirit."

"I don't understand."

"That is not important right now. I will tell you about that later. We have talked enough for today."

"But I haven't told you about what happened after George gave me the message."

"That too is not important right now."

Having said that, he turned abruptly and headed toward the village.

"Wait!" I yelled.

Flying Eagle ignored me and walked away.

❦ 28 ❦

"Why did you end our discussion so abruptly yesterday?" I asked, when I saw Flying Eagle the next morning.

"There are things that you do not yet understand. You think that things need to be finished. They do not. You thought that you needed to come to an understanding about what I was telling you regarding victims but obviously you did not. And you did not finish telling me about George. That frustrated you, did it not?"

"Yes, it did."

"Why?"

"Why?" I repeated, surprised by his question.

"Yes, why? Why were you frustrated?"

"Well, obviously, because you walked away before I was finished."

"And you had no control of that?"

"I tried to stop you so we could finish our conversation."

"But I left anyway."

"Yes, you left anyway. Flying Eagle, what are you trying to tell me through all this?"

"That what happened to you yesterday is what you fear most from the Spirit whom you can not control."

"Tell me more."

"You are afraid that the Spirit will interrupt you and prevent you from finishing what you set out to do. The Spirit has control over your death. You do not. The reason you want so desperately to control the Spirit is so you can control death. It is death that is your greatest fear and it is death that you want to control above all else. The reason you were so frustrated when I ended our conversation yesterday was that you had to face the feeling that our conversation might never be completed. That thought frightens you but you push the fear deep inside and experience it consciously as a feeling of frustration instead.

"Conversations do not have to be completed, and people do not have to finish their work, and life in the physical realm of existence does not have to go on without interruption. Death is real. It is part of life. And when it comes, it brings its own sense of completion. Do not fear death. It is a part of life."

"It is easy to say not to be afraid of death, but I *am* afraid of it and everybody I know under the age of 70 seems anxious to avoid it."

"I did not say not to avoid it. I said not to fear it. The two are quite different. When you fear death you lose personal power. When you avoid death you gain time. Coming to an early end has no value in itself. But neither does living a long meaningless life. Life is to be experienced and lived to the fullest; and, when death comes, it comes.

"But I wish to get back to something you just said. You said everybody you know under the age of 70 is anxious to avoid death."

"Yes."

"What about those over 70?"

"Well there is no magic about the age 70 itself, I just used that figure because I do know some people who are elderly who don't appear to fear death and who actually seem to be looking forward to it."

"Have you asked any of them why?"

"Yes. They said, in one way or another, that it was because they had already lived a full life. They said they were ready to die and they seemed at peace about the prospect."

"What makes them different from you?"

"I think the main difference is that I don't feel I have lived a full life yet. There are things that I still want to get accomplished and I don't want anything to interrupt that."

"So, in part, it is the fear of incompletion that causes you to be afraid of death."

"Yes. That and the fear of losing control."

"But the elderly people you have talked to about death, are they as fearful of losing control as you are?"

"No. They don't seem to be."

"And why is that?"

"I'm not sure, but I guess it has something to do with feeling that they have already accomplished what they need to do."

"Exactly! They already have a sense of completion and therefore death is not the threat to them that it is to you."

"So what are you trying to tell me, Flying Eagle?"

"That you can have the same sense of peacefulness about death now by experiencing your union with the Spirit. Experiencing the union brings a sense of completion and takes away the fear of death."

"Do you mean that after I experience the union there is nothing more for me to do with my life?"

"No. I don't mean that at all. But once you have experienced that union which already exists, all things fall into perspective and the fear of dying in a state of incompletion is gone. One can still choose to finish certain things, or to take on new projects, but one does not need to do so in order to be complete. One can be in a state of inner completion in the midst of external things that are not complete.

"Does that make sense?"

"Yes, it does."

"Good. Now, Screaming Hawk, we can get back to our conversation of yesterday.

"Our greatest role as victims comes when we are victims of death. We do not have control over death. But we do have control over incompletion. The victim chooses incompletion and puts his attention there in order to avoid facing his power struggle with the Spirit for control. The victim is afraid of the awareness of control. He seeks control and seeks to hide his desire for control all at the same time. By pretending he is out of control of his life he gives himself the illusion that he is not in control of what happens and that whatever happens is the Spirit's fault. By blaming the Spirit for what is happening, the victim tries to manipulate the Spirit into doing what the victim wants. The victim demands that the Spirit straighten out all problems and cause events to happen in a way that is consciously pleasing to the victim. But the Spirit looks on the heart of the victim and sees that the victim is not really interested in external events working out. The Spirit sees that the victim actually wants control of the Spirit above all else. The Spirit merely continues to be the Spirit, continues to be beyond the victim's control and the victim continues to construct events in his life in such a way that things do not work out well. The victim thinks that if things get bad enough the Spirit will rescue him. But if the Spirit were to rescue the victim simply because the victim has created gigantic problems, the Spirit would be falling into the trap set by the victim. The victim and the Spirit are locked in mortal combat, and the only way out is for the victim to give up and take control of his own life, instead of trying to control the Spirit."

"Why are you telling me all this right now?"

"Because that is your problem, Screaming Hawk. You are a victim. You try to control the Spirit by not controlling your life. You often choose, as you did in that bar, simply to watch and to listen, to let events unfold without your participation in the outcome. When you do not take control of your life, things do not go well for you and you feel abandoned by the Spirit. The anger you have within comes from that source. When you deal with the issue of control, you will no longer experience that inner anger and you will be at peace.

"Last summer you kept telling me that you wanted to be a man of peace. But you cannot be a man of peace until you deal with your inner anger. And you cannot deal with your inner anger until you deal with your need to control the Spirit by being a victim. It is that simple. You must take charge of your life and stop trying to control the Spirit. Only then can you lose your fear of death and truly be peaceful. Some seek to be men of peace because they are afraid of death. The true man of peace seeks peace because it is the way of the Spirit, not because it is safe. The way of peace is dangerous. The way of peace is the way of yielding to the Universe. But it is a way of yielding that is profoundly different from being a victim."

"I am surprised by your teaching today, Flying Eagle. I wasn't prepared for it. I hadn't been seeing myself as a victim or as trying to control the Spirit."

"I know. But you are in the role of victim and have been. It affects you far more than you know. Your life lacks power. And you will die in your struggle for control of the Spirit unless you yield and take control of your own life instead. That is your task. That is the task of any warrior but it is your task in particular. Take it on. Establish your boundaries of control and let the Spirit be the Spirit. Only then will your life work properly and only then will you have your full power as a warrior. That is your task, to be yourself and to let the Spirit be the Spirit. That is all."

"That's enough."

"Yes, Screaming Hawk, that is enough of a task for anyone. But for you, it is the only task there is."

❧ 29 ❧

The conversation with Flying Eagle about being a victim continued to trouble me deeply. Part of me wanted to ignore what he had said about my being a victim, but another part of me kept questioning; what if Flying Eagle is right? What if I am in the role of victim and just cannot fully recognize it?

I decided to ask him about it the next time we met together.

"Flying Eagle," I started, "the last time we talked..." But he interrupted me.

"When are you going to tell me about the rest of your encounter with George?"

I was surprised.

"I didn't think you wanted to hear about it," I said.

"I don't."

"If you're not interested, why are you asking me about it?"

"I don't need to hear about it. I am already complete. But you need to tell me about it because you are not complete. I am not giving you permission to tell me about George; I am asking you a question. When are you going to finish telling me about your meeting with George?"

"I don't understand."

"Of course you don't. Victims never understand. That is part of the way they get through life giving the appearance of not being in control."

"But I really don't understand. You are asking me to tell you about my encounter with George but you don't want to hear about it."

"No, I am not asking you to tell me about George. Because you are a victim, you need me to ask you to tell me about George. I am not doing that. I am only asking you *when* you are going to do it."

I was still feeling confused and I must have looked it.

He continued. "You thought that you had to have my permission to tell me about George, didn't you?"

"Well, yes, I guess so."

"That, my friend, is the role of the victim. Victims always think that they have to have permission to be themselves. It is not enough for them just to be themselves and do what is important to them. You, Screaming Hawk, want to tell me about George. That is because the meeting with him was important to you. You should not be concerned about offending me. You should do what you need to do."

"But I don't want to be rude by telling you something that you don't want to hear."

"Of course you don't, because then you might appear to be responsible for my boredom."

"Well, I really don't want to bore you."

"But you do bore me. Nothing is more boring than a person who is trying not to be boring. And you are trying not to be boring instead of trying to be yourself."

"But I would be boring if I told you something that you did not want to hear."

"No. When you are yourself you are not boring. It is when you are trying not to be yourself that you are boring. Tell me what interests you. But do not do it to interest me. That is boring. I hate people who try to interest me. I am not interested in anything that anyone tells me to interest me, but I am interested in everything that I am told by a person who is being his true self. You are interesting. Your maneuvers and manipulations to get my permission for you to be yourself are boring, very boring.

"Be yourself! Express yourself! If you do that, I will not be bored even if what you are telling me is of no interest to me. When people are being themselves they are never boring.

"So, Screaming Hawk, when are you going to tell me more about your meeting with George? I am not interested in hearing about it, but I want to know when you are going to tell me about it."

"Tomorrow, Flying Eagle. I'll tell you about it tomorrow."

"O.K. I still do not want to hear about it, but I will expect you to tell me about it tomorrow."

❧ 30 ❧

The next day I went looking for Flying Eagle to tell him about my meeting with George. But each place I went I was told that Flying Eagle had been there and had left a few minutes before my arrival. It was not long before I became suspicious that he was deliberately making it hard for me to find him. I then started looking in the places I thought he might go if he were deliberately trying to hide from me. Same pattern. At each place I was told that he had left just a few minutes earlier.

I decided to lay a trap for him. I went back to his room again. I figured that if the latest , "Who Done It?" he had been reading was still there, all I had to do was wait beside it and sooner or later he would go into withdrawal and come back for it.

No such luck! The novel was gone. I figured that he must have taken it with him.

I was left with only one great remaining weakness of his to exploit. It was Running Deer's week to cook again. I went to the dining hall and settled in to wait for him. To my surprise he did not show up for lunch. Half way through the meal I went to Running Deer and asked her if she had seen Flying Eagle.

"Yes," she said, "about 11:30 A.M. he showed up and said that he had some important things to take care of on the forest trail. He asked if I could feed him early. I made a plate for him and he ate here in the kitchen. He left a little while ago. When he left, he told me that you would eventually come here looking for him and that when you did, I was to tell you that 'hawks and eagles fly.' That's all he said."

I left the dining hall immediately and headed up the forest trail as fast as I could go. After about 30 minutes I caught sight of Flying Eagle up ahead on the trail. I called to him. He looked back and saw me but continued on around a bend in the trail. I ran up the trail and around the bend but when I got there all I found was Flying Eagle's mystery novel lying on the ground. I called his name again. There was no answer. I looked down the long straight stretch of trail in front of me and into the trees on each side. No sign of him. I checked to see if he might be hiding behind a tree, but I quickly noticed that all the tree trunks in that portion of the forest were too small in diameter to hide a man.

It was then that I caught sight of a large eagle making a pass over the trail just above the tree tops. I was sure it was Flying Eagle.

I felt frustrated. Once more he had managed to elude me.

Then I remembered his words to Running Deer. 'Hawks and eagles fly.' If I could not entice him to come to me, perhaps I could still go to him. I quickly sat down on the trail, closed my eyes and, following a process I had learned the previous summer, let my mind go blank. I experienced a period of nothingness, then the transition as I became a hawk. Flapping my wings, I leaped into the air and flew off through a gap in the trees to join Flying Eagle in the air.

He said nothing when I flew up to meet him. We circled together for a few minutes, climbing higher and higher in the sky. I enjoyed the exhilaration of being a hawk once again and feeling the wind flowing over my wings. I felt wonderfully alive, free and whole.

Eventually, Flying Eagle dove toward a small clearing. I followed him down and landed a few feet from him. Almost instantly he turned back into a man.

At first I had some difficulty remembering what I needed to do to change back into human form, but soon remembered that it was much like the process of becoming a hawk. I closed my eyes, yielded to the nothingness, and woke up lying on the ground next to Flying Eagle.

"How long was I asleep?" I asked as I moved into a sitting position.

"Not long, perhaps a minute. As you know, you will not fall asleep when you get more accustomed to making the transition. But at your current level of experience a minute is not bad, not bad at all."

Then he paused and looked at me.

"Why are you here?" he asked in mock innocence.

"You know why I'm here, Flying Eagle. I'm here to tell you about George."

"But I'm not interested in hearing about George."

"Obviously. I have been chasing you all over the place for the last five hours."

"Really?"

"You know I have. I have been everywhere in the whole village looking for you and it was no accident that you had left right before I arrived at each place."

He smiled slyly.

"Flying Eagle, why have you been running from me?"

"You know why. I don't want to hear about George."

"It's more than that."

"Well, actually, I thought you needed to get in touch with your own determination again. If I made it too easy to find me, you would not have had to demonstrate your determination. Victims are not determined. They let events control them. To be spiritually mature one must be able both to go with the flow of events and to determine their outcome. Part of your identity as Screaming Hawk is your determination to follow the path that is right for you. But you have not been doing that lately. You have been relying too heavily on me and you have not been following your own sense of inner direction. Your spirit knows the way to develop your true spiritual nature. As your teacher, my job is not to tell you the truth but to remind you of the truths that you already know. You must look within for direction with as much determination as you have been looking to me. You could have been a victim of my lack of interest in hearing about George. You could have been a victim of my elusiveness when you searched for me today. But you were determined and it was your determination that led you to me and that allowed you to become a hawk once again. Without determination you are not Screaming Hawk. Without determination you are a victim and you are boring.

"You are here to tell me about George. I still am not interested. But if you are determined, my lack of interest will not stop you from telling me about George and, if you are determined, I will not be bored by you even though I am not interested in what you have to tell me. Think about that. I'm going for a walk."

He stood up. I grabbed him by the ankles and wrestled him to the ground.

"Damn it, Flying Eagle, you are not going anywhere! You are going to sit here and listen to me tell you about George if I have to kill you to keep you here!"

A big grin spread across his face.

"Very good, Screaming Hawk! That's determination! I'm proud of you. You did learn something in that bar after all.

"I am not interested but I will listen. I will listen unless you lose your determination and start boring me. If you do that, I will change back into an eagle and fly away from here and you, my friend, will have to walk home because, without determination, you cannot become a hawk again."

For the next hour and a half I talked, and he listened. I told him about the rest of my conversation with George and some of my thoughts about the things George had said. Flying Eagle sat in silence. Finally he spoke.

"You said you think the man to whom George gave a ride is really Star Man. What do you make of George having found some other truckers who have also given that man a ride?"

"Flying Eagle, what interests me the most about it is that none of those men would be considered religious by conventional standards. None of them go to church or have any interest in church, and, according to George, they all live pretty rough lives. None of them are religious and yet each of them has met Star Man and was profoundly moved by him.

"It makes me question what church is all about. These men all found the hitchhiker, Star Man, Jesus, outside of church and have had no contact with organized religion since. The Church through the centuries has been proclaiming that the Church is important, even necessary. One of the early Christian doctrines was that `outside the church there is no salvation.' But if people, like those truckers, can find and relate to Jesus outside of the Church, what is the importance of the Church?"

"When you say 'the Church' what do you mean?"

"I mean organized religion, denominations, regular worship services conducted by clergy, that sort of thing."

"I see. And George and the other truckers who have met Star Man are not involved with that kind of church?"

"That's right."

"What kind of church are they involved with?"

"They aren't. That's what I have been telling you. They don't go to church, any church, and don't have any interest in doing so."

"I wonder about that. The problem may be in your definition of church."

"What do you mean?"

"Your definition is too restrictive. You say that George and the other truckers who have met Star Man do not attend church. I suspect that they do. Do the truckers who have met Star Man ever get together with each other?"

"Well, yes. As a matter of fact, George said that every now and then they all get together and discuss their experiences with the mysterious hitchhiker and talk about what he told them. They are planning to get together at the bar this Saturday night. After I told George about my experience with Star Man, he invited me to join them."

"You, my friend, have had an invitation to go to their church."

"Their church?"

"Yes, their church. Are you going?"

"I've been thinking seriously about it. I would like to go."

"Why?"

"Because it would be interesting, but more than that, because I tend to re-experience the power of my own encounters with Star Man when I am around people, like you and George, who have also met him."

"For the encounters with Star Man to stay alive for you, it is necessary to interact with others who share your experience of reality. It is in that sense, *church*

Screaming Hawk, that there is no salvation, no wholeness, outside of the Church.

"After I met Star Man many years ago and saw his wounds and realized that he is Jesus, I thought for a while that I should leave the ways of my people and become a Christian myself. During that period I read a lot of books about Christianity. In my reading I found three different approaches to Christianity. Each approach has its own implied definition of the Church.

"The first approach sees Christianity as primarily a moral, ethical system. In that approach people try to relate to the Spirit through proper conduct. They think of Christians as people who behave in certain ways and follow the ethical teachings of Jesus. Church to them is the gathering of people who share those same ethical standards and look to Jesus primarily as their teacher and model for behavior.

"The second approach sees Christianity as a system of facts, beliefs and understandings about the nature of God. The Spirit is thought to be encountered through learning, understanding and believing the right doctrines. In that approach, Christians are defined as people who believe certain things. The church is thought of as the gathering of people who share a common body of information about Jesus and have similar beliefs and understandings about him and about God in general.

"The third approach sees Christianity from an experiential perspective. The reality of the Spirit, Star Man, Jesus, is experienced directly. Ethical conduct and beliefs about Jesus are seen as valuable but far less important than the direct experience of Jesus' reality. That third approach tends to see church as the gathering of people who have experienced the reality.

"You are in that third approach to Christianity. George and the other truckers who have met the hitchhiker seem to share that third approach as well. They gather to talk about the reality of their experience with Jesus. For those who have met him, it is necessary to meet with others in order to keep that experience alive. By gathering with others and actively remembering their encounters with him, the reality of those past encounters is experienced anew and the presence of Jesus is sensed within the group that is gathered. Some theologians have called that the Real Presence. In the earlier years of Christianity, people tended to refer to the experience of Jesus' presence within the group as 'experiencing the Body of Christ.' Having that experience of the Presence with some regularity was considered essential for maintaining an awareness of the reality of the resurrection and continuing one's development toward wholeness. At first, the body of assembled belivers was seen as the vehicle for encountering the Real Presence. Later, through a misunderstanding, the church shifted the focus in its services to the bread and wine as the vehicle by which the Real Presence is encountered.

Jesus refered to the bread and wine as his body and blood, but many Christians misunderstood what he meant. They have assumed that the bread and wine are changed first and then through receiving them that the people are changed. That is not how it happens. Everything is changed at the same time. The bread and the wine are changed when the people are changed. As the people enter this new system, reality is shifted and they become the Body of Christ. The bread and the wine also become the Body and Blood of Christ because in the new system all of nature is an embodiment of the Spirit.

"By focusing on the bread and the wine instead of focusing on the people, undue importance was placed on the content of the ritual itself. People tended to deal with the ritual as a formula that could be followed in order to experience the Presence. When they started dealing with the ritual as a formula, it lost much of its power. One must always look beyond the form of a ritual to discover its true power."

"I'm not sure I understand what you mean by looking beyond the form of the ritual."

"One must think of the ritual as an expression of relationship instead of a formula to attain relationship. In all rituals the relationship precedes the actions of the ritual. In Christian worship, for example, the bread and the wine need to be received as an acknowledgment of the group's having already become the Body of Christ. Receiving the bread and the wine is not the way the group becomes the Body of Christ; it is the way the group *expresses* that reality. Is that clear?"

"Yes, I think so. But you have been talking about Christian worship from a purely experiential approach. What about the people who follow the first or second approach to Christianity?"

"They experience worship in a different way. For those in the first approach, worship is primarily a reminder to follow the principles of right conduct. For those in the second approach, worship is a time of affirming mutually held beliefs. Both approaches yield a sense of community but only the third approach leads with any frequency to an encounter of the Real Presence. Do not be confused, the Presence is always there but it is those who approach worship from the third perspective who are most likely to recognize it and respond to it."

"What about that group of truck drivers? You say that they are a church, but as far as I know they don't practice any rituals. Don't churches usually have some kind of ritual?"

"Yes. All religious groups have rituals. Any group that has met more than two or three times is usually in the process of developing and using rituals, whether they realize it or not. If you look carefully I suspect you will find that the truckers have their rituals also. In some way they will be expressing their group experience in symbolic actions.

"The best rituals are performed with awareness and intention. But rituals can be enacted without those performing them being fully aware of the significance of their actions. The power of the rituals is that they speak the language of the heart. Through them, the Spirit communicates directly with the deeper levels of our being and we in turn communicate back to the Spirit without translating our message into words. In your society much value is placed on words, but it is the actions, not the words, that are most important in rituals. The actions are far more powerful than the words. The words speak only to the mind. The actions speak to the heart.

"When you Christians celebrate communion, words are used in the ritual; but it is the actions, taking the bread, breaking the bread, eating the bread that speaks to the heart. The words declare the intention of the ritual but when the actions are performed without the words the ritual is just as powerful. That is why the Jews had prohibitions regarding with whom they could eat a meal. Even if they did not say the words of the blessing over the bread and wine at the meal, they were still performing a powerful ritual. Eating a meal with a friend is far more than simply consuming food together.

"Many Christians put emphasis on the importance of saying grace at meals. Some say the words but are oblivious to the power of the meal itself. The words have little importance. The act of eating the meal has tremendous importance. The Spirit renews us in the act of eating in ways that go far beyond the physical realm.

"Speaking of eating, Running Deer is cooking again tonight. Let's walk back and work up a good appetite. That woman is a marvel in the kitchen. I think she could take lizards and porcupine quills and turn them into a gourmet meal that would have the whole village screaming for more. Every time she cooks I am aware of our great wisdom in building that dining hall."

Flying Eagle started searching the area all around him.

"Where did I put my book?" he muttered to himself.

"You left it on the trail when you changed into an eagle."

"Oh. In that case, I will pick it up on the way back. I must have laid it down without realizing it. Usually anything that a person is wearing or holding goes with him when he makes the transition to animal and then back into human form again. But not always.

"I remember hearing a story once about Flying Hawk," he said as we headed back toward the trail. "He was a good medicine man in most respects but he was very vain. One day, after he had changed into a hawk and was flying over the forest, he noticed a group of women from another village who were gathering berries in a meadow. He decided to fly down and astound them by turning back into a man right in front of their eyes. They were astounded all right; when he turned back into a man he discovered that he had left all his cloths behind. It was very embarrassing. He was so flustered by the event that he couldn't turn back into a hawk and had to run back to his village naked."

"He sounds a lot like somebody I have met. Are you sure his name wasn't Flying Eagle?"

"No! Definitely not! But I failed to mention that the same experience can occur with those who are disrespectful to their elders. After that last comment you made, Screaming Hawk, I would suggest that *you* pick *your* landing sites very carefully."

❧ 31 ❧

The time for my return to the college was now only two weeks away. I had a sense of excitement and challenge about reorganizing the department and developing the new, experientially oriented, curriculum. But I was also feeling disappointed that I would, for the most part, be working on the project alone. I knew from experience the loneliness of bringing forth new projects without a partner to share their joys and frustrations.

My repeated attempts to contact the third candidate were unsuccessful. I had written to him at his address in Nebraska and had left messages on his telephone answering machine several times. His recorded message simply said that he was "on the road again," and to please leave a message so he could return any calls when he returned.

"Flying Eagle," I said, as we walked together in the forest, "I really want to fill that opening at the college. There is a lot of work to do. I need the help but, even more than that, I need someone to share in the process. I need someone to bounce ideas off of, someone to get excited with me, someone to gently tell me when an idea I have is crazy. The prospect of working alone on the reorganization of the department is not very appealing to me.

"But time is running out. I have done everything I can to fill that position on short notice. I can't get in touch with that third candidate. I have racked my brain for people I know who are appropriate and might be available. I can't come up with anybody. I called the college president yesterday to see if he had come up with anybody else. He has advertised the position and made a number of calls to other schools and to people he knows. He said that he has a few prospects who might be worth interviewing for next year but no one else who might be available this year. I don't know what else I can do."

"Just one thing, Screaming Hawk."

"What's that? I'll do anything."

"Do nothing."

"That's your answer? 'Do nothing'?"

"Yes. You have already done everything you know to do. Now trust the Spirit. If the Spirit wishes you to have a partner for this project, and you do not block the process, one will be provided. You have done your part. Now your job is not to block the will of the Spirit by being anxious about it. The will of the Spirit usually unfolds through circumstances. But your anxiety generates forces that tend to create events that conform to your expectations. Your anxiety is an expression of your expectation that you will not find anyone. Let go of your anxiety so the Spirit can create through circumstances."

"O.K."

We walked on in silence for a while.

"Today is Saturday," he said. "Are you going to go to that meeting with the truckers tonight?"

"I have been feeling anxious about the amount of work I have to do to get ready for the fall semester. I have been thinking seriously about skipping the meeting tonight and getting a head start on the planning."

"You are operating out of your anxiety, Screaming Hawk"

"I guess you're right. I do want to go to that meeting."

"Follow your heart, Screaming Hawk. What does your heart say?"

I paused. "It says to go to the meeting."

"Then go. Your work can wait. At times one can do more work by doing nothing."

❧ 32 ❧

When I walked into the smoky bar, George gave me a wave from a table at the far end of the room. Three other men were already seated with him.

"Am I late?" I asked, as I walked over to the table.

"Nope. Right on time." George motioned to the vacant chair at their table. I sat down. "Hope you don't mind sitting back here. This is the quietest corner in the place."

Bill, Harry and John introduced themselves to me by first names only. I did the same. The atmosphere was friendly and relaxed.

A waitress came over to the table and asked me what I wanted to drink. I noticed that the men had been sharing a carafe of wine which was already sitting on the table. I decided to join them. The waitress brought me a glass and left.

George looked at me and said, "We were talking before you arrived. I was telling them that you met someone in the forest a while ago who sounds a lot like the hitchhiker."

I told the group about my encounter with Star Man the previous summer and about the second brief meeting I'd had with him on the trail this summer. A couple of them nodded slowly as I talked.

When I finished, John said, "Yeah, that sure sounds like him. When I met him he wasn't wearing Indian clothes but everything else you described, the wound in his hand, the kind of things he said to you, all sound like the hitchhiker to me. When I met him he talked to me about love too and said some of the same things to me that he said to you. I only met him once, a few months ago, but I sure would like to meet him again. I've never felt so peaceful as when I was talking to him."

The next to speak was Bill, a large man, nearly as large as George, with a round jolly face and a beer belly that almost touched the edge of the table.

"It's interestin' that he talked to the two of you 'bout love. I've met him three times and he didn't say nothin' to me 'bout love. Each time I talked to him he talked 'bout kids. Well now, come to think of it, in a roundabout way, maybe he did talk 'bout love. He sure did love kids. He told me lots of funny stories 'bout kids and things they said or done. That's all he talked 'bout each time was kids.

"Some of his stories made me do a lot of thinkin' 'bout how many child support payments I've missed and how long it's been since I've seen my kids. I sent my ex a big check to make up part of what I was behind and I've been makin' extra payments since. I'm only three months behind now. I've started callin' my kids regular too. I call 'em ever' week now. I don't say much to the ex; we still ain't on speakin' terms, you might say. But I talk to my kids, and they tell me 'bout school and ever'thing they's doin'. Ever' Saturday we talk on the phone. Last week my boy had a problem at school and he called me to talk 'bout it. Made me feel real good.

"All that's happened since I met the hitchhiker. He never told me to call my kids or nothin'. In fact, he didn't talk 'bout me at all. Ever' time I've picked him up he got in the cab and right away started talkin' 'bout kids. He talks and talks and we laugh together 'bout some of the things kids do; and that's it. Then he says that it's time to let him out. So I stop my rig and he gets out. I've never seen his hand or nothin'. So I don't know 'bout that wound you guys talk about, but he did say something kind of peculiar like. When I asked him if he had any children of his own, he said, 'More than you could ever count in a lifetime,' which was kinda weird, but I had a strange feeling that he was telling the truth. That's all he said 'bout himself. But like you guys, I started to wonder if maybe he was Jesus or somethin'. Now I'm pretty sure that's who he is."

"I don't know who he is," said Harry, a dark haired, leathery-skinned, man in his late 50's. He took a quick, nervous, drag off one of the cigarillos he was chain smoking and continued. "All I know is that he is the strangest person I've ever met. He told me things about myself that nobody, I mean *nobody*, else knows. Kind of gave me the creeps. He talked about some things I had done in the Navy that I'm not proud of. And he reminded me of some other things I'm not very proud of either. Told me that I'm wasting my life and that if I don't change my ways that I'm going to die lonely and miserable with nothing to show for it except some illegitimate children that I've never met.

"Hell, I don't know why I'm telling you guys this stuff. You seem to like him. I don't. I only came along because George told me about meeting the hitchhiker and said that you guys meet to talk about your experiences with him. Well, I'm here. I'm here because I'm so God damned confused by the things he told me that I can't sleep nights. I wish I'd never met him. If I can just figure out what he's up to maybe I can put him out of my mind and get on with my life.

"So you guys talk. I'll listen. But I can tell you right now, I don't like any of this. I'd rather be spending my time with a good woman who won't let me sleep all night, instead of staying awake thinking about what that damned hitchhiker said."

No one spoke for a minute. Then George said. "Harry, I don't know why he decided to speak to you. And I'm sure that some of the things he told you were disturbing. But I want you to know that you are welcome here and that anything you have to say is O.K. with me and that it's also O.K. to just sit and listen. Everybody that's here has been affected by the hitchhiker in some way. We are all different in some way because we met him. We are here to talk about it and for some of us, like you, to figure out what all this means. All I know is that meeting him was the most important thing that has ever happened to me. I'm still trying to sort this all out too, but I'm convinced that he is Jesus and that he met each of us because he loves us. Beyond that, I don't understand much more than the rest of you.

"So hang in there, Harry. If I can be of any help to you, just ask, and if not, maybe you can help the rest of us figure out what this is all about."

John looked at George intently with his intense dark eyes, "You said you think he met us because he loves us. Why do you say that? What he said to Harry doesn't sound very loving. Sounds pretty judgmental to me."

"I think," George responded, "he was probably concerned about Harry and that's why he said what he did.

"What do you think, Harry?"

"I don't know. But I don't like it! I don't like anybody telling me how I live my life!" He shot a short blast of smoke in the direction of the ceiling, for emphasis, and snuffed out the stump of his cigarillo with a couple of quick angry stabs into the overcrowded ash tray.

"Well I don't know," John responded. "If the hitchhiker really is Jesus, he doesn't fit the image I had of him as a kid. Now I could see him going around talking to people about love. But I can't see him getting tough with people like Harry describes."

"Well I can tell you this," Harry muttered as he lit another cigarillo. "He acted just like that God damned son of a bitch'n goody two shoes Jesus that Billy Jones' mother told me about the time she caught me and Billy reading sex magazines in the shed behind their house. I didn't want anything to do with a Jesus like that then and I sure as Hell don't want anything to do with a God damned hitchhiker Jesus now."

"Sounds like you think the hitchhiker is Jesus," I observed.

"Well maybe I do, and maybe I don't."

"What's the part that makes you think that he is Jesus?" I asked.

"It was the look in his eyes when he said I was wasting my life. He looked like it really mattered to him." Harry was speaking more slowly now and his lower lip trembled slightly as if he were starting to relive a powerful moment. Then he collected himself abruptly and continued. "Shit, nobody ever gave a flying fuck what I did with my life except that Mrs. Jones and now that damn hitchhiker." His speech slowed again when he mentioned the hitchhiker. "Ah shit, I'm so fuckin' confused now I don't know what to think."

"It sounds to me," said George, "like you have met Jesus, corny as that sounds, just like the rest of us. And that he gave you a clue to his true identity when he came to you in the only form that you would recognize, as the Jesus that Mrs. Jones described. The rest of us experienced him in somewhat different ways, but all of those ways, including yours, Harry, seem to me to have been expressions of love. Maybe that's what this is all about. Love in all its various dimensions coming to us in human form."

We continued our discussion for another hour and a half. Harry remained quiet most of the time but did make an occasional comment. It was George who started drawing things to a close by saying, "Getting together with you guys and talking about the hitchhiker this evening has meant a lot to me. In a strange way it feels like I am with him again; that he is here, not in any one of you alone, but present in all of us as a group. And that includes you Harry. I feel his personality here just like I felt it when I was talking to him in the cab of my truck.

"I'm going to be on the road for two weeks, but I could meet here three weeks from tonight."

Bill and John nodded their agreement.

"I'll be leaving before then," I said, "but I want to thank you for including me in the meeting tonight."

The group looked at Harry. He looked down for a moment as he weighed his decision and then looked up.

"I'll be here," he said softly.

"Good," said George. The others smiled their agreement.

"I know some of you have to start driving pretty early in the morning," he continued, "but, before we go, I wonder if we could acknowledge the hitchhiker's presence with us tonight in a special way." He started pouring what was left of the wine into each of our glasses.

"I'll pass," said Harry, and then added, "But maybe next time."

George nodded and skipped over Harry's glass. Then George broke a pretzel in pieces and gave each of us, except Harry, a piece. He said, "When Jesus was with his disciples he ate and drank wine with them. He has been here tonight. Let's eat and drink this in remembrance of him."

We ate our piece of the pretzel and finished off the wine in our glasses. That was all, and yet doing that seemed far more important than just eating pretzels and drinking wine. I, too, had felt his unmistakable personality present in the group. The pretzel and the wine represented his physical body, but in an even more profound sense, we, the group, had become his body. He seemed to be alive again in us.

As we were walking out to the parking lot George put his hand on my shoulder. "I got your message," he said.

"What message?"

"The message you left on my answering machine in Omaha. I'm on the road so much I don't get back there very often any more. I have a friend there who checks my machine for me and calls to give me any messages left on it. He's been out of town for more than three weeks but he's back now and he gave me a call right before I left for the meeting tonight. The message said to call you at the Indian reservation. I didn't know your last name until I got the message but I figured it had to be you."

"You are George Olson?" I was in shock.

"That's right," he said smiling. "Guess you didn't recognize me in my uniform, " he said, fingering his 'T' shirt. "Don't let that fool you. When I was teaching philosophy of religion I weighed 50 pounds less, didn't have my goatee and used to wear a coat and tie every day. Women used to think I was the cat's meow. I used to pass up opportunities that Harry would give his eye teeth for. But look at me now, fat and happy."

He chuckled, then looked serious again and continued. "The last time I picked up the hitchhiker he told me that it was time for me to go back to teaching. I said, 'No way! If I have to go back to that coat and tie crap.' He said that he had some pull and could 'make arrangements.'"

"The coat and tie are negotiable," I said. "Let's go back inside. We have a lot of talking to do."

❧ 33 ❧

I arrived back at the village about 3:00 AM and went directly to bed. I was awakened about 10:00 A.M. by Flying Eagle's gentle, barely audible tap on my door. Instantly, I was fully awake.

"Are you awake?" he asked in an equally soft whisper.

I smiled.

"Of course I'm awake!" I boomed. "How could anybody sleep with somebody pounding on their door like that!"

I got up quickly and opened the door. When he saw the unmade bed and that I was still in my pajamas he became uncharacteristically flustered.

"I'm sorry. I did not mean to disturb you if you were sleeping."

I grinned broadly.

"Come on in. I was up late, but I have already slept longer than usual. I wouldn't have heard you unless I had been ready to wake up."

He relaxed noticeably. I motioned him to the only chair in the room. He sat down in it. I sat on the edge of the bed.

"Screaming Hawk, sometimes life gets more exciting than a good mystery novel. I have been waiting for this next chapter as patiently as I could, but I can't wait any longer. I want to know if you offered George Olson the position."

I was astounded.

"You knew who he was?"

"I guessed. When you have been tangling with the Spirit as long as I have, you know that one of his favorite stunts is to keep putting what you are looking for right under your nose. The Spirit finds that amusing. I don't, but the Spirit does for some reason. Now that I'm on to that little stunt, the Spirit doesn't use it on me any more, but I figured that you probably hadn't learned that lesson yet.

"When you first told me that you had met a man named George, I figured he was probably the one you were looking for in Nebraska. The Spirit is sly, very sly."

I told Flying Eagle all the details of my meeting with the group and about my discovery that George was indeed George Olson.

"Flying Eagle, we went back into the bar and talked for three hours. He is exactly what I have been looking for. He loved teaching but quit five years ago because the administration kept insisting that all his courses be totally academic. He looked for a while for a school that would allow him to teach the material with an experiential approach, but didn't have much success. He started driving a truck to support himself because a local trucking firm was short handed and offered him a job. He loved it and has been driving ever since.

"We talked about my ideas for the new curriculum for an hour and put more together in that time than I could have done on my own in a week. We work beautifully together. He's got strengths in the areas where I'm weak and vice versa."

"So you offered him the job?"

"Does Screaming Hawk scream? Of course I offered him the job, and he accepted, on two conditions. First, that he not have to wear a coat and tie to class, and second, that he be allowed to get a job driving a truck on the week ends or school breaks if he wants to. I'm sure I can get the administration to agree to that. And he can start work three and a half weeks from now. It's perfect."

"Screaming Hawk, the reason you found him was that you yourself have become able to encounter religion experientially. That made you free to bring into your reality a candidate who could do the same."

"By the way, did you recognize any rituals during your evening with the truckers?"

"Yes. When we ate the pretzel and drank the wine it was like having communion."

"At what point did you recognize that as a ritual."

"When George broke the pretzel and gave it to us to eat."

"But you were eating pretzels and drinking wine throughout the meeting; were you not?"

"Well, yes. Come to think of it, we all were, even Harry."

"All of you, including Harry, were involved in the ritual even before you recognized that it was a ritual. Eating and drinking is always a ritual. You are always receiving the life giving Spirit when you eat and drink. The words are not important. Recognition of the ritual is not important. The ritual exists without words and without recognition. The ritual is in the actions. And it is in those actions, the rituals that we perform, that we receive life.

"The gradual changes that you noticed in Harry as the evening progressed did not occur as a result of anyone's words. They occurred because the Spirit was present in your midst as you ate and drank with him. The words were there at the end of the meeting but the words were unimportant. The Spirit comes through our actions. Always remember that. Words are for the mind. Actions are for the heart and for the Spirit.

"Let's take a walk."

I dressed quickly. Then we headed into the forest as we had done so many times before.

"You will be leaving soon," he said. "In the days that remain before your departure there will be very little new teaching."

"But Flying Eagle, there is still so much that I want to learn. I want to know more about the Path of Illumination and the Path of Indifference."

"You will learn more about them, but that will come later. Some of what you learn, the Spirit will teach you directly; other things, I will tell you when you return. But now you are in danger of learning too much that goes beyond your level of experience. Those who do that can become dry and academic. You must spend time absorbing and practicing what you have learned here this summer. There will be time for more learning later.

"The warrior must work on his spiritual journey as hard as he works at defending the boundaries. You are a warrior. You are about to return to your world of teaching others how to experience what they already know in their hearts. You must do the same. Practice what you know in your heart. Practice the Paths. Follow your inner urges and come to recognize the gentle nudges of the Spirit. All these things must be done if you are going to effectively teach others to experience the Spirit.

"It is also time to start preparing for your departure. A physical journey means saying goodby to people and to places. It takes time to do that properly. You need to say goodby to the people of the village who have become important to you. You must say goodby to the land and to the trees in the forest. You must say goodby to the animals. They are more a part of you than you yet realize. And you and I must say goodby.

"Many people do not say goodby well. They assume that they are taking who they are with them and that life will go on as before, but that is not the case. Part of who you are will remain here long after you go. You must say goodby well so that the part of you which stays behind will in time be free to leave and return to you."

"What do you mean, the part that stays behind?"

"When people leave a place they always leave part of themselves behind. That is why traveling can be so tiring emotionally as well as physically. Places hold far more importance than those of your culture usually recognize. When you are in one place for a while your spirit attunes itself to what is present in that location; attachments are formed and your spirit can then draw power from that place. When you leave a place, it takes time for those attachments to be broken and for your full power to be returned to you. A warrior on a journey always has less power than he would have defending his own territory. Some of your power now comes from the earth, the trees, the animals and the people of this place. Other power comes truly from within you. Both kinds of power are important and, to be most effective, you must have both. Those who say goodby poorly leave much of their power still attached to the place. In some cases it can take many months or even years for that power to return to them. Those who say goodby well take more of their power with them and the rest returns to them more quickly.

"Take time now, over the next few days, to walk down these trails. Say goodby to all that you see, to the trees, the animals, even the rocks; they too are important. Start saying goodby to the people of the village. Prepare well for your departure.

"Saying goodby is like dying. Those who are dying must say goodby to this realm as they prepare to enter the next. They must prepare to leave past attachments behind and to take their power with them. When they do not do that properly and remain too attached to people or places in this world, they can not take enough of their own power with them to operate effectively in the next world. They may become ghosts for a time, until they have sufficient power to break free of this realm and fully enter the next. Learn from them. Say goodby now with your heart. Feel the pain now, so you can take most of your power with you when you leave this place."

We walked on in silence for a long time. As we walked I started saying goodby in my mind to all the things that we passed. Grief welled up within me and tears dropped here and there along the trail.

❧ 34 ❧

The process of saying my goodbys continued over the next days. From time to time I felt intense grief, as I had on the trail. At other times saying goodby was pleasant and meaningful. I made a deliberate effort to speak with each person in the village and spent more time with those I knew particularly well. True to his word, Flying Eagle covered very little new material in our sessions and spent much of the time we had together reminiscing about experiences he had as a youth and in his early training as a medicine man. On some occasions I talked to him about the waves of grief I was experiencing and about how important he had become to me. At other times we merely walked together through the forest in silence.

Four days before my departure we met as usual for our time together. I noticed that Flying Eagle was looking dismal. He said nothing for a long time. I assumed that he too was feeling grief over my upcoming departure and would talk about it with me when he was ready. Finally he spoke.

"I learned only this morning that Buffalo Woman will be returning to the village tomorrow."

"Is that what's been bothering you, Flying Eagle? And all this time I thought you were feeling upset about my departure."

He ignored my comment and continued, "It is worse than that. Not only is she coming back, but she has made arrangements to start cooking again on Saturday."

I laughed.

"You may think that's funny, Screaming Hawk. You are leaving that day. I have to stay here and endure a whole week of that woman's culinary abuse. I'm not prepared for this. When she went to visit her cousin, I had hopes that she might decide to live there permanently and my torment would be over. I don't know how she does it but that woman can merely boil a pot of water and it will come off the stove unfit for human consumption."

I laughed again. Flying Eagle did not.

"Screaming Hawk! This is serious. I don't want to have to eat another thing that woman fixes. I have had it with her! I should have had her thrown off the cooking schedule months ago."

"You really are serious about this; aren't you?"

"Yes, I'm serious. That woman and her cooking makes me furious. There is no reason why I or anyone else should have to endure any more of it."

"Flying Eagle," I started, half in jest but also half in seriousness, "a few days ago you told me that eating any meal is a ritual, whether we recognize it or not. Is it also a ritual to eat meals that Buffalo Woman has cooked?"

"No."

"Why not?"

"It's not! That's all there is to it!"

It was obvious to me that pressing my question any further was only going to make him more angry with me. I decided to leave it alone.

A few minutes later Flying Eagle announced that he was going back to his lodge. I didn't see him the rest of the day.

❧ 35 ❧

The next morning Flying Eagle was still in a foul mood. Attempts on my part to joke with him were met only with hostile glares.

"You are still upset about Buffalo Woman; aren't you?" I said.

"Yes. I have done a lot of thinking about it and it is time to do something. I am going to go to her and tell her to stop cooking for the village. I should have done that a long time ago."

"Wouldn't it make sense to have one of the other elders who is not so upset with her go and talk to her about the situation?"

I got another glare from him.

"No." He said flatly.

Attempts to talk about other subjects were equally fruitless. I decided that it was not the right time to return to our discussion about my grief over leaving and the special pain I felt over leaving him. I left him and visited the last of the villagers to whom I had not yet said goodby.

Later that morning Buffalo Woman arrived by car. The driver, a man in his 30's, who appeared to be a relative, assisted the portly woman in unloading her belongings into her small house. Then he gave her a brief hug, said goodby, and drove away.

Flying Eagle paced nervously some distance away, apparently giving her a few minutes to get settled before going to talk to her. I went over to speak to him but he ignored my presence and continued walking back and forth deep in his own thoughts and obviously still angry. After about ten minutes he crossed the road and went to her dwelling. Buffalo Woman met him at the door and invited him inside. I sat down under a tree and waited for him.

Twenty minutes later he emerged looking shaken. He noticed me under the tree and headed over in my direction. I stood up and walked over to meet him.

"Are you alright?" I asked, feeling deeply concerned about him. He looked stunned and gazed out ahead of him as though he were not quite fully aware of his surroundings.

"Let's walk," he said quietly without looking at me.

I steered us in the direction of one of the forest trails. We walked slowly, side by side. A few minutes later he spoke.

"I was not prepared for this," he said, still looking straight ahead.

"What happened?"

He stopped walking but continued gazing off into the distance.

"She has met Star Man."

"Really?"

"I was angry. I went to tell her that she is not a good cook and should not be cooking for the village. She told me that she already knows that she is not a good cook and that she does not want to cook for the village. She said that it is painful to her to know that people do not enjoy the food she fixes for them. She knows that some of the people tell stories about her and laugh. Many times, she said, she has wanted to quit but is not able to do so."

"Why not?"

"Because Star Man told her to cook for the village. He came to her and said that he wanted her to be a cook in the dining hall. She argued with him about it. She said that she had never been a good cook and that she had tried many times to learn to cook well but that she was not able to succeed. Star Man said that was the reason that it was important for her to cook. He said that some people in the village had grown accustomed to life being easy. He said that the people had forgotten what it was like many years ago when the food was scarce and they were grateful for anything that would sustain life. He told her that people now acted like it was their right to have meals the way they wanted them and that they had forgotten that all food is a gift from the life giving Spirit. He warned her that she would be ridiculed by some of the people and that they would not understand. He asked her if she was willing to endure that.

"She told him that she was not a strong person and that it was very painful to her when people were not kind to her.

"He said that she must suffer but that he would not allow her pain to go beyond that which she could endure.

"Screaming Hawk, she cried as she was telling me this. I remembered all the things I had said about her, the stories I had repeated about her and the contempt that I had felt for her.

"In my religion we put much emphasis on respect, respect for the Spirit, respect for the earth, respect for the animals and respect for other people.

"I have not respected Buffalo Woman. Star Man chose her to do a far more difficult and painful task than he has ever asked of me and I ridiculed her because I did not understand."

Tears were streaming down his face.

"How could I have been such a fool? I teach the people the importance of respect but I have not been respectful of one of my own people.

"And I have ignored Star Man's own teaching to me. He told me that all meals are a gift from the Spirit and that to eat any meal is the deepest of all the rituals given to us by the Spirit. I ignored that. I put myself above the Spirit when I told you that eating Buffalo Woman's meals is not a ritual.

"I realize that I am one of those who has grown to expect the Spirit to be revealed only in the easy life. I have not been thankful unless the food has tasted good and I have failed to recognize the gifts that the Spirit has given me. He has given me food that I have not appreciated but he has also given me Buffalo Woman, a person of great courage, and I ridiculed her. I contributed to her pain.

"I begged her to forgive me.

"She did. But I cannot forgive myself."

He crumpled to the ground and sobbed bitterly on his hands and knees, then lowered himself further until he was lying like a dog with his face resting in the leaves.

"Leave me now. I must face this pain alone."

I left him on the trail and returned to the village alone, humbled and shaken.

❧ 36 ❧

I entered the forest in the afternoon and spent time alone in silence. Then I returned to the village and visited Buffalo Woman.

She received me warmly and graciously. I made no mention of her conversation with Flying Eagle but told her that I had grown to deeply respect her and that I would miss her. She seemed pleased and wished me well on my journey.

"I will cook something for you," she said. "It will not taste good. I am not a good cook. But I want to give you something for your journey tomorrow."

I was touched and felt deeply honored.

"I would like that."

I gave her a hug and left her home.

Late in the afternoon I happened to see Flying Eagle emerging from the forest. As I walked over to him I could see that he was at peace again.

"Screaming Hawk," he said, smiling broadly, "Star Man came to me in the forest. All is well."

"What happened?"

"I was in deep pain. I felt humiliated. I grieved a long time. All the cruel things I had said about Buffalo Woman and her cooking kept going through my mind. Over and over I cried, 'I have been such a fool.' Then I felt a touch on my shoulder. At first I thought that you had returned. I was going to tell you again to leave me in my grief. But when I looked up I saw that it was Star Man. He said nothing. He just held me while I sobbed. Then he was gone.

"I have never felt such love for me. I know that he knew all about Buffalo Woman and that he also knew that I had distorted his teachings about food. I am not deserving of his care but he loves me anyway. He has forgiven me and I can now forgive myself.

"I wish to ask your forgiveness as well."

"That's alright. I never believe anything you tell me anyway," I said with a smile.

He made a mock expression of total exasperation with me and said that my last comment had removed any lingering doubts he might have had about it being time for me to leave. Then he paused, became serious again and said, "No, you misunderstand, Screaming Hawk. I was not asking your forgiveness for telling you that eating Buffalo Woman's meals is not a ritual. That is between me and Star Man. He has forgiven me for that. I wish to ask your forgiveness for not sharing openly with you about my own grief over your departure. You have shared your feelings with me. I have not yet expressed my grief to you.

"You have become like a son to me but you have also become my brother, my friend and my colleague. I have shared many things about the Spirit with you. You have listened; you have learned; and you have applied my teachings. We have grown close in the process and we can now talk together about the Spirit in a way that I have done with no other except with my own teacher years ago. You have filled a void in my life that was left when my teacher died. We now have that special kind of bond that I have with no other living person. My heart is breaking because you are leaving but I did not tell you that. Instead, I talked about Buffalo Woman and I have filled these last few days together with my broodings and talk of my anger at her. I ask your forgiveness for that. Our relationship deserves better treatment and you, my brother, son, and friend, deserve to know my deep feelings for you."

I looked deep into his eyes and said, "You are forgiven."

For a long, eternal, moment he gazed back absorbing what I was offering him. Then he said, "That is good."

He looked around and sniffed the breeze.

"Enough talk," he said. "It's time to eat."

We headed off in the direction of the dining hall.

"This will be your last meal with us for many months. I have made special arrangements. A warrior should eat a good meal the night before his journey. I used my influence and got Running Deer on the schedule. At the time I thought I was making arrangements for your journey but in a strange twist of fate the Spirit has arranged that this is also my last meal before I embark on a spiritual journey of 'eating crow,' as you say in your culture.

"Buffalo Woman will start cooking again tomorrow. I have new respect for that woman. To have equal respect for her cooking may take me a little longer. The Spirit really got me this time! Now I have to receive Buffalo Woman's cooking as a ritual. And if I complain about it to anybody, I thereby demonstrate my own lack of spiritual development. The Spirit is laughing at me." He looked up at the sky, shook his fist and shouted, "Go ahead, laugh! Have your fun! But I'll get back at you! I'll..." His expression suddenly changed from mock rage to brilliant insight and then ecstasy.

"I have it!" he exclaimed, looking at me. "This time I have it!"

He looked back at the sky, raised his fist again and shouted, "This time I've got it! You didn't like my working crossword puzzles? You haven't seen anything yet!"

He lowered his fist. He smiled; he grinned; he chuckled; then he roared with laughter.

"I'm brilliant! Absolutely brilliant!" he shouted and then roared with laughter again.

"What are you going to do?" I asked when he paused a moment to catch his breath.

He just looked at me with a sly smile plastered across his face and said, "It is a secret. For now it must remain my secret. But the time is coming when the Spirit will have to treat me with new respect."

We arrived at the dinning hall and had a wonderful meal with the people of the village. That night Flying Eagle and I laughed and told stories and celebrated our time together. I went to bed feeling happy and fulfilled, thanking the Spirit for the opportunity of knowing Flying Eagle and the people of the village.

❧ 37 ❧

I was up before dawn packing and loading the car. About daybreak Flying Eagle came out to say goodby.

"I will miss you," he said. "Be careful on your journey.

"Today you have many, many miles to travel. Long trips are tiring and difficult. Today I must eat Buffalo Woman's cooking. I figure the difficulty of our tasks is about equal."

I laughed. "Flying Eagle, you haven't changed."

"I know. I am still having trouble with my new task. But now I know that there is value in enjoying a bad meal. I will find a way and in the meantime only you will know how difficult it is for me. To the village I will appear to be a great warrior having conquered another challenge with ease."

At that point Buffalo Woman arrived carrying a paper bag. Flying Eagle greeted her with genuine warmth.

"I have baked some muffins for you to take on your journey," she said to me.

"Thank you," I said taking the bag from her.

"Have a good trip," she said and departed.

"I have genuine respect for that woman now," Flying Eagle said. "But be careful! Eating those muffins will be a real test of your courage.

"There is one more thing that I wish to confess to you. I have told you many stories. You may share any of them with your students. You may also share the story about Flying Hawk's being naked when he changed back into a man. It has much value as a story about the danger of having too much pride. But what I am going to share with you now you must not tell another living soul. If you do, I will never tell you another thing and I will devote all of my remaining days to making your life totally miserable.

"That story was about me. I was Flying Hawk."

I laughed. "I knew it! It sounded just like you."

"Now get out of here," he shouted, "before I change my mind and decide to kill you to protect my secret!"

I drove away laughing. My grief was gone and I took most of my power with me.

After a few winding miles I glanced at my watch. It was time for breakfast. This morning Buffalo Woman was serving the meal to Flying Eagle and some of the braver souls in the village. I thought of them as I opened the bag and ate one of the muffins. It tasted awful. But it was wonderful. As I ate, and they ate, we all shared in communion together.

I laughed and I had a feeling that, this time, Flying Eagle might have been laughing too.

Just after I turned onto the main highway I saw a familar looking torch red Stingray convertible approaching at a high rate of speed. The driver, her golden hair flying in the breeze, braked hard and turned down the road to the village.

"Oh my!" I muttered, "the young woman from Chicago. Poor Flying Eagle! It looks like the Spirit isn't finished with him yet."

And the Spirit laughed hard and long.

❧ About the Author ❧

Patton Boyle grew up in Charlottesville, Virginia. In addition to writing books about the path of spiritual growth and discovery, he has worked for a number of years as a pastoral counselor/psychotherapist and, as an Episcopal priest, has served congregations in the United States and in Mexico. His first book, *Screaming Hawk*, has been published in English, French and German. The author may be contacted through Station Hill Press, Station Hill Road, Barrytown, New York 12507.

Also Available from Station Hill

A Journey to the Ancestral Self
The Native Lifeway Guide to Living in Harmony with Earth Mother
TAMARACK SONG

"For the deer and the grasses I have written this book, so that we may again be At One with them." Thus writes Tamarack Song, in this extraordinary, practical guide to native lifeways — the essential wisdom connecting all native peoples. Though the author is white, the book speaks to readers from every background who seek a connection with their essential self — that person, deep within each of us, "who dances to the Drum around the ritual Fire, who knows healing lore from times when plants spoke, who yearns for the peace and Blessings of walking again in the Balance of Our Earth." In clear but evocative language, the author shares his unique message: that the lifeways of all Native peoples are essentially one, sharing not just the same ceremonies and life transitions, but the same spirit and reverence for life; and that all of us, regardless of ethnic background or religious upbringing, are essentially Native people. The book begins by demonstrating how native lifeways— the ways of the Guardian Warrior, the caretaking of children, reverence for elders ("Keeping the Ancestral Voice"), and many more — are intrinsic to the human experience. Drawing on a series of native traditions — from fasting and feasting to dreams and the receiving of visions — the book then shows the reader how to bring to life those intuitive, sensory, and spiritual powers that have been long-hidden and little used.

Tamarack Song founded Teaching Drum School to pass along native lifeways in a wilderness setting. He lives in Three Lakes, Wisconsin.

$14.95 paper, ISBN 0-88268-178-8, 6 x 9, 264 pages, 11 graphs, 20 drawings, bibliography, index.

WALKING THE ROAD OF VISIONS
WITH MY LAKOTA GRANDMOTHER

MARY ELIZABETH THUNDER

Thunder's Grace

MARY ELIZABETH THUNDER

A part-Indian woman who was searching for her roots found much more ... acceptance of a Mother. Abandoned by her real mother when she was three weeks old, Mary Elizabeth Thunder survived abuse, a broken marriage, and a death experience during an operation after a heart attack to become a self-actualized woman leader and teacher. The late Grace Spotted Eagle, who asked Thunder to write this book for all women to know no matter how hard their life has been, they too can have a life that is full of love, laughter, and joy working itself out of the dysfunction perimeters through ceremonies. Thunder's story is the true tale of a remarkable elder, Grandma Grace Spotted Eagle, who adopted her and guided her in a spiritual awakening as a messenger. At once harrowing and uplifting, this memoir takes us from Thunder's early life and experiences with legendary elders such as Grace Spotted Eagle, Wallace Black Elk, Rolling Thunder, and Chief Leonard Crow Dog, through the death experience that utterly transformed her, to over nine remarkable years she spent traveling America by van, culminating in her inclusion in the Sun Dance, one of the world's oldest and most venerable initiations on the North American Continent. Intimate, painfully honest, essentially and overwhelmingly spiritual, this is a book about a woman's quest for meaning amid two cultures and a compelling account of the visionary side of Native American life.

Mary Elizabeth Thunder, is a well known Speaker, Human Rights Advocate, Sundancer, Peace Elder, Mother, Grandmother, and Wife of Native and Non-Native descent. She has traveled globally now to share a message of Peace and healing of the earth by healing of oneself. She and her husband Jeffery Hubbell live and maintain a ranch which is a Spiritual University in West Point, Texas.

$14.95p, ISBN 0-88268-166-4, 256 pages, 40 b&W photos.

ORAL TEACHINGS BY THE VERY VENERABLE
KALU RINPOCHE

Gently Whispered

*Oral Teachings by
the Very Venerable
Kalu Rinpoche*

Foreword by H.E. the XIIth Tai Situpa

This compilation of teachings presents the oral wisdom of Kalu Rinpoche, revered worldwide as a teacher of Vajrayana Buddhism. Here are his views on the mastery of the three *yanas*, the vows of Refuge and Bodhisattva, and the true nature of the mind. Also included are techniques for stepping beyond the Four Veils of Obscuration and Emotional Subjectivity onto the Five Paths that culminate in the liberation of *mahamadra*, plus a thorough introduction to the visualization techniques of *yidam* practice, a detailed commentary on the *Chenrezig sadhana*, and an extensive explanation of the Bardos of Death and Dying. Leavened with humor and fresh insight, this first English translation is an excellent resource for the novice and experienced student alike.

Kalu Rinpoche (d. 1989), a celebrated teacher of Tibetan Buddhism, was the head of the Shangpa Kagyu lineage and founder of numerous Kalu Rinpoche centers around the world.

$15.95 paper, ISBN 0-88268-153-2, 6 x 9, 304 pages.

Wonders of the Natural Mind

*The Essence of Dzogchen in
the Bon Tradition of Tibet*

Tenzin Wangyal

Foreword by Lopon Tenzin Namdak

The Bon are the indigenous, pre-Buddhist natives of
Tibet, and *Wonders of the Natural Mind* is the first
introduction to the popular Dzogchen philosophy
from the Bon perspective, fully compatible with the
major Buddhist teachings. For the growing number
of Westerners interested in Dzogchen, Wangyal ex-
plains the specific meaning of the teachings, and
takes the reader step by step through their practice.
He covers both meditation and the visionary aspects
of Dzogchen previously regarded as secret.

Tenzin Wangyal is a *geshe* (the Tibetan equivalent of professor) with many years of
experience under Lopon Tenzin Namdak, head of the Bon lineage. Formally trained in
India, Nepal, and Norway, Wangyal has set up a teaching institute in Charlotteville,
Virginia, and is presently at Rice University in Houston under a Rockefeller Fellowship.

$14.95 paper, ISBN 0-88268-117-6, 6 x 9, 256 pages.

Self-Liberation Through
Seeing With Naked Awareness

*An Introduction to the Nature of One's Own Mind
in the Tibetan Dzogchen Tradition*

**Translated and edited, with introduction and commentary
by John Reynolds
Foreword by Namkhai Norbu**

This is the first authentic translation of *The Tibetan Book of the Great Liberation*, a fundamental classic on personal transformation that is derived from the same "treasure text" as the *Tibetan Book of the Dead*. Once poorly translated by Evans-Wentz, this new version by a celebrated Tibetologist reveals clearly what is said in the original text. The nature of Dzogchen, not a philosophy or sect but the primordial state of every individual, transcending intellectual and cultural limitations, is discussed at length in John Reynolds' extensive commentary, based on the oral teachings of Namkhai Norbu Rinpoche, Lama Tarchen Rinpoche, and his Holiness Dudjom Rinpoche.

$29.95 cloth, ISBN 0-88268-058-7, 6 x 9, 240 pages. Order No. P0501, $14.95 paper ISBN 0-88268-050-1

The Cycle of Day and Night

*An Essential Tibetan Text on
the Practice of Contemplation*

NAMKHAI NORBU

Translated by John Myrdhin Reynolds

Namkhai Norbu clearly presents the ancient tradition and includes instruction in contemplative practices that are integrated with activities in both waking and sleeping states. Based on a teaching by Garab Dorje, the first human master of the Dzogchen lineage, this book gives a translation of the author's Tibetan text, together with a commentary drawn from his oral explanations.

Namkhai Norbu Rinpoche is a Tibetan Lama who, from 1964 until the present, has been a professor of the Oriental Institute of the University of Naples, Italy, where he teaches Tibetan and Mongolian languages and Tibetan cultural history.

$10.95 paper, ISBN 0-88268-040-4, 5½ x 8½, 128 pages.

Death is of Vital Importance
On Life, Death, and Life After Death
ELISABETH KÜBLER-ROSS, M.D.

Five intimate, conversational talks, edited from speaking engagements, offer an overview of the life and work of a woman who has been as influential as she is remarkable. Enlivened with dozens of striking case histories and memorable stories from the author's own childhood, the book recounts such events as her extraordinary meeting with a woman in the German concentration camp of Maidanek a few months after the war, here mother's death, and her own near-death experience and epiphany of "cosmic consciousness." Also included is a step-by-step breakdown of the experience of dying, descriptions of the differences among physical, psychic, and spiritual energy and of her method for interpreting children's drawings, based on Jung's theory (and later expanded by Dr. Bernie Siegel). She offers insights into the now-famous story of Dougy, the young boy whose question "Why do little children have to die?" led her to create the best-selling Dougy Letter, and proposed the establishment of ET (elderly-toddler) centers, where children can be "spoiled rotten." At the end of this special book, readers will feel that they have spent a privileged evening in the presence of a wonderful and very wise woman.

Elizabeth Kübler-Ross, author of the international bestseller *On Death and Dying,* has been one of the most prominent pioneers of the hospice movement. Her farm near Staunton, Virginia, is also a retreat and workshop center.

$12.95p, ISBN 0-88268-186-9; 216 pages, 6 x 9, bibliography.